D1460575

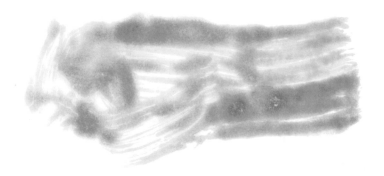

OFF TO WAR WITH '054

OFF TO WAR WITH '054

John Kemp

Merlin Books Ltd.
Braunton Devon

ISBN 0 86303 459-4
Printed in England by Antony Rowe Ltd., Chippenham, Wilts.

FOREWORD

Throughout the Battle of Britain and during the next four years aircraft of Fighter Command were controlled by a complex radar network with high masts dotted on our coastline and underground operations rooms. For the invasion of Europe, however, there was a requirement for mobile radar systems that would not only give our fighter leaders vital information about enemy formations but, like our fighter wings, would move across Europe immediately behind Montgomery's armies.

The author, himself a fighter pilot in the Battle of Britain, tells the story of how his small forward radar unit sailed across the Channel on D-Day plus five and set up his equipment on the beachhead. A few days later, on 15 June 1944, I led 144 (Canadian) Spitfire Wing to our first airfield in Normandy, St Croix sur Mer, and both our units became part of the Second Tactical Air Force in France where we found the controlling equally as good as that previously provided by Fighter Command; we immediately gained complete air superiority over Normandy, isolated the battlefield by destroying road bridges and rail centres and blasted any moving vehicle on the French road and rail networks.

A few weeks later we left the bocage country and began the long haul across north-west Europe to be halted by Montgomery's failure at Arnhem (where the controlling was superb), the Rhine and the onset of winter. But in the following spring it was soon all over.

For many of us the Normandy invasion and the subsequent trek into Germany was the most exciting period of our young lives and the author gives us a fascinating account of how we lived and fought during those momentous days.

Air Vice-Marshal J. E. 'Johnnie' Johnson
CB, CBE, DSO(bars), DFC(bar), DL

CONTENTS

	Foreword	5
	List of Illustrations	8
	The Ballad of '054	9
1	15054 FDP	13
2	Controlling	18
3	Renscombe Down	27
4	Chigwell	32
5	Blue Group	38
6	Last Preparations	46
7	Off to France	54
8	Normandy in June	58
9	Static	66
10	Moving on	73
11	Brussels and Beyond	83
12	Air Battles over Nijmegen Bridge	92
13	Winter	104
14	In the Ardennes with USAF	114
15	Final Moves	122
16	Travemünde	128
	The 15054 Chorus	138

Appendices
1	Technical Equipment	139
2	Personnel	141
3	The Convoy	142
4	Itinerary	143
	Glossary	144

ILLUSTRATIONS

Set between pp.72 & 73

Type 15 search radar with IFF interrogator — and Type 13 nodding height finder
Type 11 search radar aerial
Type 15 radar Operations/receiver vehicle on Crossley chassis Type 13 height finder aerial packed 'ready for the road'
A 'flash' photo of the PPI teller
Exterior of Type 15 Receiver/Operations vehicle (Type 409)
     . . . and the interior
Quote from Montgomery's 'Normandy to the Baltic'
Combat report of destruction of ME 262
Page from an 83 Group Daily Intelligence Summary
Author on VE Day at Travemünde
Bill' Jones who kept everything working
All of us at Travemünde
The 'Hard' Travemünde looking east towards the Russian Zone
The Baltic coast just off the base at Travemünde
Travemünde — Blohm and Voss 138 flying boats
     — 'Any more for the Skylark?'
     — The giant BV222 with an FW190
     — One of our mini submarines
Corporal Bluett's watch of radar operators outside Type 11 vehicle
A V1 store near Leck
The first Fokke Wolf 190 off the '054 assembly line
Belsen — survivors
     — non-survivors

THE BALLAD OF '054
by
Ian Beith

From far and wide the countryside
    In bright bow ties and breeches,
In bowler hats and some in spats,
    And some in rags and stitches,

They left their posts and came in hosts
    To serve their king and country,
They came to report as any man ought
    Who's got four limbs on his gantry.

And some were enlisted and some were conscripted
    And failed were a lucky few;
They dressed them neat in a suit complete
    Of beautiful Air Force Blue.

And out on the square in the cold wintry air
    Each morning they made them parade;
They marched them about in column of route
    And then finally taught them a trade

They taught WT, Radar Op. and MT,
    And how to prepare a stew;
They set a trade test, selected the best
    And formed them into a crew.

Then from coast to coast, from pillar to post
    They travelled up hill and down dale;
Till aboard a small ship, on a watery trip
    The valiant crew set sail.

For battle prepared, the Channel they dared,
    The Armada of '054;
To the bridgehead they hove and courageously drove
    Up a quiet but battle-scarred shore.

They selected the site, then with vigour and might
    Set up their mysterious gear,
And midst flak thick and hot did unflinchingly plot
    With the courage of Boadicea.

When a Hun came in sight there ensued such a fight,
    Due entirely to '054
Ere an eyelid was batted, the hostile was shattered
    To add to their glorious score

And the *Luftwaffe* fled as the crew surged ahead
    On a cross-Continental tour;
And the *Luftwaffe*'s might was smashed in the fight
    Of the fabulous '054.

Till this band of Crusaders, these noble invaders,
    Invaded Der Vaterland,
And with fervour inspired, much booty acquired,
    And lived on the fat of the land.

With our heavy guns rumbling, the Wehrmacht was crumbling
    We watched their defeat on the Rhine;
And with skill unsurpassed did plot to the last,
    An example that ever shall shine!

Till at last they announced that the Germans were trounced
    And as any amongst us will tell,
Though the war they'd survived they somehow contrived
    To outlive VE-Day as well!

For with liquor imbued such fighting ensued
    As never had been seen before;
And with riotous feast now the battle had ceased
    They drank to the end of the war.

Now again on the square, neath an officer's care
    Once again they all have to parade;
And in column of route they marched them about
    In uniforms somewhat frayed.

And 'What lies ahead?' is in every man's head,
  Are they bound for the Japanese war?
With the realization, demobilization
  Won't be for a year or more!

So they all have to wait the decision of Fate,
  When in bright bow tie and breeches,
In bowler hats and some in spats
  And some in rags and stitches,

They return to their posts, demobbed in hosts,
  Having served their time without fear;
And no more shall roam but build a new home
  And start a large family to rear!

The small parade of rather less than forty men that comprised 15054 at that time was lined up in front of me dressed in blue battledress. I had just been introduced to the men as their new Commanding Officer. I looked steadily at the airmen running my eyes along the ranks curious to know what sort of unit I had inherited and I came to the immediate conclusion that they were a poor looking lot, scruffy, sullen and unmotivated. They in turn looked back at me with a variety of expressions, mostly it seemed with indifference, some with curiosity and a few with open hostility.

It was in the early summer of 1943 that I first met up with No. 15054 AMES (Air Ministry Experimental Unit) at Chigwell on the north-east outskirts of London. Royal Air Force Station Chigwell was the home of the giant Base Signals Unit that was responsible for the formation, manning, equipping, training and supporting the vast number of RAF Signals Units large and small that were sent overseas during the 1939-45 war. 15054 was one of those units.

It was a bad start to our relationship. Together we were to carry out more than a year's arduous training in England before crossing to Normandy with the invasion forces in early June 1944. We were to lead the ground forces of the RAF Second Tactical Air Force across France, Belgium, Holland and Germany and celebrate VE Day at the giant *Luftwaffe* base at Travemünde only yards from the Russian border.

Thinking back I now know that I was very prejudiced. I had just been posted away from 15061 AMES that I had commanded since its formation. '061 had been a similar type of signals unit to '054. It was equipped with radar supported by ground to air and ground to ground radio so that it could detect and report back air activity both enemy and friendly and also control defensive and offensive fighters. The unit was planned to be very mobile with specially designed equipment and a minimal but highly trained crew. It was intended that it should operate as far forward as possible in order to obtain the maximum coverage over enemy territory. '061 had been trained to a high standard and as a result its morale had been excellent. I was confident that when the time came the unit under my command would do a good job. It was not to be, '061 was suddenly detailed for special convoy protection work in the Mediterranean. The cooks, clerk, drivers and admin personnel were no longer required, the officers were replaced.

The appointment as Commanding Officer on such a unit was a secondary task, my main function was that of senior fighter controller or GCI controller as it was then known. The word radar had not then come into general use, the UK designation was radiolocation but as that was in itself secret units were known by the initials of their task, e.g. a GCI station was the title for a Ground Control Interception unit. There a controller with the aid of his crew worked directly from the radar display guiding fighters by orders and information transmitted to the pilot by radio telephony to a successful interception of enemy aircraft by night or day.

Personnel who worked on the new equipment, such as operators, mechanics and fitters were given the letters RDF (range and direction finding) as a prefix to their general trade designation. However, in this story they will be referred to by their modern equivalent, e.g. radar fitters and so on.

I had originally applied to join the RAF in late 1937 during the time of the great expansion of the armed services and after the usual selection board at Air Ministry at High Holborn I was accepted for pilot training in the Class A Reserve. This meant a year of full time training and I was ordered to report in early January to a civilian *ab initio* Flying Training School near Perth in Scotland. My first instructor was a little Irishman who had been the leading aerobatic pilot in Sir Alan Cobham's Air Circus. I think he must have held the all time record for the greatest number of practice landings per flying hour. He would take over the controls and as soon as the Tiger Moth was airborne he would dip the port wing and pull the aircraft round just clearing the tops of the two hangars. I am sure that we never went higher than a hundred feet and with the Tiger Moth half-way round its final turn into wind I would be given the controls to sort myself out. As I tried to obey his instructions for left rudder, top rudder and more or less bank the ground came up a bit quickly. I was due for an early solo after only six and a half hours flying but there was a snag on spinning and I finished up with a new instructor. I was very relieved when a month after my eighteenth birthday I finally went solo and probably did the best circuit of my short flying career.

In March the course survivors went down to RAF Uxbridge where

14

we met up with several dozen trainee pilots from other civilian flying schools. For two weeks we were drilled on the parade ground, lectured on behaviour as officers, fitted with uniforms by London tailors and commissioned. We were then posted to our RAF flying schools. I found myself posted to No.10 Flying Training School at Ternhill near Market Drayton in Shropshire. At my arrival interview I was asked whether I would like to be trained on single- or twin-engined aircraft. I expressed my preference for twins explaining that I was very interested in navigation and long range flying and that I had obtained excellent marks in navigation at the civilian flying training school. I was rather surprised therefore when I found I had been detailed for single engined training on the Hawker Hart and Audax aircraft.

At the end of the junior term I was asked if I would like to do my Advanced Service Training as a single-engined light bomber pilot or as a fighter pilot. I expressed my interest in navigation once more and asked to go on light bomber training. I was less than surprised when I found myself detailed for fighters.

It was, looking back, a good decision as I then flew the Hawker Fury aircraft which was a delight. I enjoyed the formation flying, the aerobatics and especially the air to air and air to ground gunnery attacks. At the end of the term we were posted to squadrons and I found myself with No. 64 Squadron at Church Fenton in Yorkshire. The squadron role was that of a night fighter and it was equipped with Hawker Turret Demon bi-plane aircraft so called because the rear gunner position had a snail like wind break covering. It was a much heavier and slower aircraft than the delightful Fury and it was obsolescent. The squadron was about to change to the twin-engined Blenheim monoplane that was just coming into service,

In January as I came to the end of my year of full time service I was asked if I would apply for a Short Service commission. I had however just married and could not afford to stay in the service. Under the age of 30 I would not have been eligible for the various allowances payable to a married officer. I therefore left the RAF in January 1939 and with a background of a good science subjects schooling I was able to get a job with Vickers Armstrong at Brooklands in Surrey as a wind tunnel assistant at the magnificent salary of 3 pounds a week. In the June I did my two weeks of reserve training at Hamble on Hawker variants in the course of which I was sent on a cross-country to locate and report on the old man of Cerne Abbas.

The threat of war had been steadily growing since the Munich agreement in 1938 between Chamberlain and Hitler. As a member of the RAF Reserve I had received papers instructing me what to do in the event of a call-up of reservists. However, I was in a reserved occupation and should it happen it was unlikely that Vickers Armstrong would release me to go.

When the German forces invaded Poland I did not wait for my call-up but reported to RAF Pembrey in South Wales as detailed on my papers. The new airfield had not yet opened and there was only a small advance party consisting of a Squadron Leader, a Pilot Officer and six airmen on the station. I helped them hand out bedding and arrange accommodation for some 600 airmen and naval ratings from No.2 Air Armament School that arrived during the night.

I was soon to be moved to Scotland to join 609 (Auxiliary) Squadron at Drem for flying duties. The squadron was equipped with Spitfires and as apart from the small Magister I had flown only bi-planes, I was sent to Aston Down in Gloucestershire for a conversion course. There I flew up to five sorties a day on Harvard aircraft practising formation flying and gunnery attacks. By February I was operational on Spitfires with just over 200 hours total flying in my log book.

Following the breakthrough of the German forces in France in early May 1940, 609 Squadron was sent down to Northolt at short notice on the 26th May. The bar at the mess at lunch-time was full of pilots from other fighter squadrons recounting hair raising experiences of being shot up and shot down, of armour plate and baling out and finding the way back through enemy lines. I was not destined to fly from Northolt however as another squadron pilot 'Red' Garton and myself were pulled out of the bar and told that we were being posted immediately to No.54 Squadron at Hornchurch in East London which had lost several pilots and was short manned. We travelled together and arrived at Hornchurch that same evening and were introduced to 'Prof' Leathart the newly promoted CO of the squadron who was still wearing his Flight Lieutenant stripes not having had time to get his new rank stripe sewn on. We were asked if we were prepared to fly early the next day and were at once detailed for a sortie at 04.00. It was to be the squadron's last Dunkirk patrol.

The 54 Squadron Spitfires were fitted with the new VHF radio and the Rotol variable pitch propellers as contrasted to the fine and coarse settings of 609's aircraft. Prior to getting airborne I was given cursory instructions on how to use the new equipment. All three squadrons of the Hornchurch Wing got airborne together but none could manage to

16

raise more than nine aircraft. The squadrons split up soon after take-off and 54 flew alone toward the huge black cloud of smoke rising from the burning oil tanks at Dunkirk.

We passed a lone Lysander aircraft and later saw a single Dornier 17. Al Deere who was leading the squadron ordered the section of three aircraft that I was in and which was led by Colin Gray, to stay on guard at high level whilst the others dived down to attack, As Al turned in behind the Dornier I saw a trail of white glycol vapour coming from his aircraft where he had been hit by the rear gunner. Al was forced to crash land in France and after a few adventures found his way back to the UK on a destroyer. 'Red' Garton was lucky enough to have been detailed to one of the other sections and was able to fire his guns and claim a fifth share of the destruction of the Dornier.

I flew from Hornchurch, Rochford and Manston airfields in the south-east corner of England up to the September of 1940. I caused the *Luftwaffe* little or no discomfort although I was shot down twice and parachuted into the sea on one occasion when my engine failed whilst on convoy protection patrol. Some of the 54 pilots were later among the most highly decorated fighter pilots of the war. I acquired two small cannon shell splinters that put me off flying for a couple of weeks, qualified for membership of the Caterpillar Club for baling out of my aircraft, the Goldfish Club for being rescued from the sea and was lucky to survive the Battle of Britain.

Chapter Two   *Controlling*

When the squadron was sent up north to Catterick for a rest in September I was detailed for duties as a (fighter) controller in the Sector Operations Centre. The Sector was defended by a day squadron of Spitfire aircraft and a night squadron of Blenheim aircraft fitted with an early version of airborne radar (AI). The Spitfire squadron was 54 Squadron, now acting in a training role for new pilots prior to their being posted to the more active sectors in the south of England. The work was to give radio control to the pilots during their day to day training and to intercept any German aircraft approaching the Sector. The position and direction of an enemy raid was shown by coloured arrows and plaques indicating raid strength and height on a large coloured and gridded map that filled the floor of the operations room. The arrows and plaques were moved about by WAAFs wearing headphones through which they received the plotting information. The pilots made occasional visits to the operations room whilst I was sitting in the centre chair just to discuss things of common operational interest and at the same time to look over the range of attractive WAAFs on duty and to make some provocative remarks they could overhear.

CH stations (long range radar) sited on the coast provided information on aircraft flying over the sea and the Observer Corps reported all aircraft flying overland. All reports on aircraft from the various sources were passed to a Filter Centre that carried out a rationalization of the air picture and recognition of the tracks, passing on to the Sector and Fighter Command operations rooms only those designated 'Hostile' or 'X Raid' (Unknown), or those of special interest. The location of friendly fighters was obtained by a system of radio bearings on an automatic transmission from the aircraft known as 'Pip-Squeak'.

The major weaknesses of the system were that cloud and darkness made the work of the Observer Corps extremely difficult and the plotting accuracy and time delay made it impossible to position the night fighters near enough to the enemy aircraft for them to be picked up on the airborne radar which had a maximum range at the time of their height above ground, say about two miles. Attempting to intercept aircraft at night was at that time very frustrating and the only light moments were when the controller thought he had got the night fighter near enough to the enemy for it to show on the aircraft AI and he gave the coded call to the pilot 'Flash your weapon'. The only results I ever obtained were smirks, or blushes, or giggles, from the WAAF listening in to all that went on.

I liked the work of directing the fighter pilots and was nominated to attend No.2 Course at the newly formed Fighter Controller school at 'Woodlands' a large house in Stanmore, Middlesex, known to all as Windy Joe's after the CO. It was a well organized effort with a mock-up Sector Operations Room and its GSM or general situation map on which the raids were plotted and totes showing the readiness states of squadrons, airfield weather, radio channels and so on. There was an elevated dais where the controller sat and issued his orders by radio (R/T) to the fighters. There was also a simulation triangulation room where the fighter positions were determined by simulated radio bearings and the position passed to the GSM.

To add to the realism and also to get the trainee controllers to understand a little of the distractions and difficulties faced by fighter pilots, two Walls' ice-cream box-tricycles were used. One was fitted with a large red flag to show that it was the bomber or enemy aircraft, it had an aircraft compass mounted between the legs of the rider and a metronome on top of the former ice-cream box immediately in front of the rider. In an adjacent field the 'bomber' was launched from one side of the field and the 'pilot' pedalled off on his predetermined raid headings. Three airmen stationed at points on the edge of the field regularly took compass bearings on the tricycle and passed them to the triangulation room. The operators there pulled strings across the table along the bearing passed to them. These formed a 'cocked hat' where they crossed and this position was passed to the GSM. By suitable arrangement this would be presented on the GSM as a raid actually approaching the UK sector for which the trainee controller was responsible.

When the raid was designated 'Hostile' the controller then ordered off his fighters. The second tricycle bearing a blue flag was the simulated fighter. In addition to the compass and metronome it had an R/T set which was in direct communication with the controller in the operations room. The fighter set off from his airfield which was a special point in the field which was identified as an airfield on the GSM. The controller then ordered the 'fighter' pilot to steer various headings (vectors) and 'fly' at varying speeds called 'Liner', 'Buster' and 'Gate' set by pedalling in time with the metronome. The fighter position was determined in the same way as that of the bomber and the positions passed to the GSM. As the tricycles moved across the field so the fighter and bomber plots moved across the GSM. A successful interception was achieved when the two plots were brought together which would have meant that the two tricycles had collided.

Unfortunately whilst I was at the school successful interceptions were unknown. It was very cold outdoors and the field was extremely rough making pedalling and steering the tricycles most difficult. To adjust the pedalling rate to a metronome setting was impossible. To steer by compass, pedal and use the R/T at the same time was beyond the capabilities of most of the trainee controllers. It was no uncommon sight to see the 'Fighter Pilot' get off his machine, take off his headphones and then lift the back wheel of the tricycle off the ground and move the machine around until the required compass heading could be achieved

I was finding the course of great interest and was upset when a signal was received telling me to report to the BBC at Daventry for an introductory course prior to training as a signals officer. At this time there was a desperate shortage of signals officers and this took priority over aircrew duties for those educationally qualified. I found no difficulty in absorbing the elementary radio background of tuned circuits and feedback and so on but I felt I would be of far greater use to the war effort using my fighter pilot background as a fighter controller. I put my case to the Chief Engineer and composed a letter for his signature. I was soon called to Air Ministry where some very angry words were said to me by a senior signals officer, but he finally agreed to release me and I was then posted to the newly formed 9 Group covering the fighter defence of NW England.

I had an interview with a Group Captain on arrival at the Group Headquarters where I expressed my wish to work on to the new highly secret equipment that would enable the successful interception of night bombers. I was then told in no uncertain terms that my wishes were of no account and I would be sent only where he decided and so on. I was duly sent to Valley in Anglesey for duties in the Sector Operations. The work there was the very routine one of looking after defensive patrols over convoys in the Irish Sea. The general standard of controllers at this time was still very low and even that simple task was more than some could manage.

Soon after my arrival at Valley one of the first prototype mobile ground Control Interception radars (GCI) arrived and was set up on the

Rhosneiger golf links with the object of intercepting the night bombers attacking Liverpool. I immediately volunteered to work on the new equipment and I am sure that the other controllers were relieved as I was the only volunteer. It was an additional pleasure to find when I reported for duty that I knew well one of the small team of officers which was to demonstrate the working of the equipment. It was Jim Bazin who had been on the night fighter squadron at Catterick.

I was shown round the line of vehicles and trailers forming the convoy. There was a receiver aerial, a transmitter aerial and two diesels all of which were mounted on trailers and a transmitter and a receiver/operations room both of which were arranged on a Crossley three ton chassis. The R/T receiver and transmitter were sited some distance away to prevent interference on the equipment. The RDF (radar) aerials appeared to me to be identical. On each aerial trailer was a turntable and mounted on it was a plywood cabin about six feet cubed. On one side of each of the cabins was a very large wooden framework about twelve feet high and twenty-four feet wide covered with chicken wire netting on which numerous half metre horizontal dipoles and feeder wires were mounted. The aerials were turned by an airman inside each cabin who sat and rotated by hand a pair of bicycle pedals connected by a driving chain to the turning system. A foot pedal in the operations vehicle worked a buzzer in the two cabins telling both airmen when to change direction of turn in order that the aerials should sweep together searching over a required arc of sky. A goniometer in front of each airman indicated when the aerials were out of synchronization and the airmen had to adjust their rate of turning until they were in unison again. There was also a telephone line to each cabin from the controller which often passed not so polite messages.

As might be expected the whole was experimental and unrefined. The controller sat in the darkened vehicle facing a cathode ray tube on which a fine coloured line radiated from the centre. This was the direction in which the aerials faced. An aircraft picked up by the equipment showed as a brightness on the line (trace) at a distance from the centre proportional to the aircraft range from the aerial. As the aerial turned so the brightness left a faint yellow afterglow on the tube. In effect the response was shown as a plan position on a map and the tube was known as the PPI (Plan position indicator). The aircraft height was obtained by an operator sitting close alongside the controller facing another cathode ray tube with a horizontal trace. The controller would call out the range of the aircraft on which he required a height. As the

21

aerial swept across the aircraft a split signal response rose out of the noise or grass on the horizontal trace and the operator had to judge from the rapidly moving response the relative length of one leg of the response against the other, e.g. 10/7 or say 9/10. By running a hinged ruler over a chart showing ranges against ratios a height could be obtained. Other operators in the controllers team read off plot positions from the PPI, calculated the target's course and speed, recorded events and maintained liaison with the Sector Operations Centre.

When enemy night bombers were plotted in the SOC and were seen to be heading towards the GCI area the GCI was ordered to alert and the equipment switched on and the aerial cabins manned. A night fighter would be sent off by the Sector Controller and ordered to call the GCI on the R/T for instructions. The controller at the GCI by using the foot buzzer to the aerial cabins caused the aerials to sweep over the arc in which the raid was expected to appear.

The maximum range at which an aircraft flying at about ten thousand feet could be picked up on the new equipment was only about 35 statute miles and the aircraft was indicated by a vague yellow looking slug of rapidly fading afterglow over some eighteen degrees of aerial turn. The actual position of the aircraft was at the centre of the inside edge of the response. As the aircraft got nearer to the equipment so the response became smaller and its centre was more easily judged especially as it also showed more clearly. The arc formed by the response always centred on the GCI itself, i.e. the centre of the cathode ray tube and it gave no indication of the aircraft direction of movement which was determined by marking in chinagraph successive positions on the PPI. However, the aircraft heading was different again due to wind drift and this had to be determined in order to place the fighter directly behind so that the fighter's own radar could pick up the raider. This meant within a distance less than the fighter's own height above ground which was often less than 10,000 feet or under two miles.

Even if everything worked and conditions were ideal a successful interception required a great deal of judgement and an element of luck. There were so many things that could go wrong. On the fighter side the weather could be too bad for the fighter to take off; the aircraft could go unserviceable; its radar fail; its R/T fail; the cloud and icing be so bad that even if the fighter closed to minimum range on its radar nothing could be seen or the bomber could take evasive action. On the GCI side the difficulties were even more numerous. The radar could develop a fault; the diesels fail; the R/T fail or water get into the cable to the R/T site. Even a little dust or dirt in the sliprings that transferred the signals from the rotating aerials or even under the foot operated buzzer that told the aerial cabin turners to change direction caused trouble.

The aerial turners after a long time changing direction back and forth often lost the rhythm and the aerials faced in different directions and no signals were received. More usually the enemy aircraft flew into the areas of permanent clutter or responses that came from the high ground of the Snowdon area and the ground that surrounded the site, or the SOC ordered the fighter to be called off because it was entering a gun defended area.

A Squadron Leader of the Auxiliary Air Force had been made the CO of the GCI, I was under training and allowed to carry out practice interceptions using two Defiant aircraft, one acting as fighter and the other as target. The real operations against enemy aircraft were carried out by the Squadron Leader using one of two of the new Beaufighter aircraft equipped with airborne radar and four 20mm cannon that used to fly in to Valley on short detachments. There had been no successes until the night of 31st May 1941 when after yet another failure to make an interception the Squadron Leader got up from his seat in front of the console, took off his headset and flung it down in disgust. I thought I saw my chance and asked diffidently, "Can I have a go, Sir?" I was told vulgarly that I was at liberty to do what I liked with the radar and radio together with a few coarse suggestions.

I sat down at the console, put on the headset and let the aerial sweep completely round in a search for enemy aircraft. To my surprise and intense disappointment all the raiders which had been heading south-west on their way home after their attack on Liverpool seemed to have disappeared until I noticed on a following sweep a single aircraft response appearing from the clutter of permanent responses formed by the mountains. I directed the Beaufighter pilot (Sqn. Ldr. Colbeck-Welch, 219 Sqn) into a position behind the raider and when in the Criccieth area he reported that he had a contact on his aircraft radar and that his radio observer was taking over. After a while he reported that he had a visual on the aircraft which was showing two small amber lights and would I check if any friendly aircraft were in the area? Sector reported nothing friendly about and the pilot said he was opening fire and a few moments afterwards told me that he had destroyed it. I learned later that the final stages of the interception were not without incident as just as I turned the fighter behind the raider the Beaufighter door which was behind the pilot in the centre of the fuselage floor had come open and was only closed with much difficulty.

The Ju 88 which crashed into the sea off Aberystwyth was the first enemy aircraft in north-west England to be destroyed by a fighter at night and was the cause of much jubilation to all but my Squadron Leader. A staff Wing Commander from Group took the pilot, his radio observer and myself out to a champagne supper in celebration. About ten days after this having been accepted as being operational on the equipment I was acting as duty controller when a raid was reported approaching from the south and a Beaufighter from the 68 Squadron detachment was scrambled. The pilot called on the R/T and I ordered him to steer 180 degrees. "Understand vector one eight zero," came the acknowledgement in a slow guttural foreign voice. I directed the fighter into a position astern one of the leading raiders and watched excitedly as the two responses merged together. I saw the single response split into two again and the pilot called, "New vector please." I decided against trying to chase after the original aircraft and directed him on to a second. I again watched the two responses merge together and then there was another call from the pilot as before, "New vector please." I directed him on to yet a third raider and watched the two responses merge. Again the call, "New vector please." By this time I had the feeling that things were going really badly. The fighter was half-way to the Isle of Man when I put him on to a fourth raider and watched the responses come together yet again. After a period of quiet there was suddenly an excited voice on the R/T, "Engine on fire, engine on fire, vector for base." I told the pilot to steer 180 for base and gave him his distance. I rang the airfield and told them to get the fire tender on top line as the Beaufighter was returning to base with an engine on fire, I thought to myself that to lose my fighter would be the final bitter blow on what had been a bad night. There was no other fighter available to try for further interceptions of the enemy raid. All of us in the GCI crew heard the returning fighter and waited unhappily a long while for information.

The telephone from the airfield rang. It was the Intelligence officer who had been trying to debrief the pilot Pilot Officer Mansfeld and his radio observer Sgt Janocek. Both were Czechs and the debriefing was not helped by their limited English. The IO then told me the great news that it was not Mansfeld's aircraft that was on fire but the last enemy aircraft that he had intercepted. He had in fact sighted all four aircraft and fired at three of them. Fighter Command the next day credited him with two aircraft destroyed and one damaged. Mansfeld was given the immediate award of the Czech DFC and Janocek the DFM. The Operations

Research department of Fighter Command in those early days required a vast amount of information on each attempted interception which included radar pick-up ranges, closure ranges, tactics, visibility, cloud conditions, evasive measures, rounds fired and so on, each of which involved about a page of questions. There was some difficulty in getting the information! Mansfeld became one of the most famous night fighter pilots of the war. He returned to Czechoslovakia after the war and then came back to the UK to rejoin the RAF, teaming up again with Janocek. I was to meet up with Mansfeld a number of times after the war.

I was very happy with the new (GCI) equipment. It was a tremendous advance in air interception to be able to control from equipment where the position of fighter and enemy aircraft could be seen at the same time in plan position and there was a facility also to determine the heights. I was convinced that it was the answer to the night and day attacks on the UK. The German night bombing blitz on London had been carried out for sixty-seven consecutive nights during the winter and had driven Londoners in their thousands to sleeping and even living in the Underground. Heavy raids on other major towns had been carried out with little successful opposition. Early attempts at night interception using radar controlled searchlights and night fighters equipped with AI had brought little success and the sending up of 100 Hurricanes during the heavy raid on Coventry brought no result.

I had more success and quickly went on to command the unit with promotion to acting Squadron Leader. I was twenty-one at the time which was even in wartime a bit young and I grew a moustache to make myself look older. There were a few more successes but the main attacks over NW England no longer approached over Anglesey. At the end of the year I was posted to the delightful unit at Hope Cove in Devon where Susan Noble, a most attractive, pleasant and capable WAAF officer was my adjutant and all unit personnel were accommodated in the Cottage Hotel in Hope Cove that had been requisitioned. The radar was sited in the middle of the advanced landing field at Bolt Head where four Spitfires were kept at 'Readiness' during the day. We were lucky when early one morning when I was on duty the airfield was bombed and strafed by a few Fw 190s who concentrated on the Spitfires and did not attack the radar, we had no casualties. I was CO of both the airfield and the GCI but the situation was too good to last and when the airfield was given its independent CO the opportunity was taken to move me. I went to another GCI at Ripperston on the coast of St Brides Bay on the south-western tip of Wales. We had some successes against the few aircraft

25

minelaying near Milford Haven or attacking Swansea and Cardiff and which wandered into our coverage.

The times of heavy night raids on the UK were over however and there were long weeks with no enemy activity. There was talk of a Second Front and I was pleased when I received orders to report to Renscombe Down near Swanage for what I hoped would be more active involvement with the war and perhaps the hoped for Second Front.

Chapter Three

Renscombe Down was where many of the small mobile signals units were formed and carried out the first stages of their training. It was a small establishment split between the two villages of Langton Matravers and Worth Matravers near Swanage in Dorset and was commanded by a squadron leader. A large house next to the rural deanery had been commandeered and this formed the headquarters and technical training centre, whilst the hutted camp at Worth provided most of the accommodation and was the home of the RAF Regiment training staff.

I was the first squadron leader to be posted in for training and was told that the course was designed to toughen-up everyone and provide the necessary training for work as mobile units in the field. I had been posted in to command No.15061 AMES Signals Unit whose role was that of a control and reporting radar. My two flight lieutenant controllers turned out to be Jerry Jacobs an ex-pilot of about my own age and Griffiths a Cambridge mathematics don. We were taken to the officers' accommodation which was a number of airmen's beds on the bare floor of a large room in the house. This was typical of the 'toughening-up' process which included very poor food and seemed to be just a cover up for poor administration.

Prior to the so called toughening-up training at Renscombe most of us trainees had been employed on Air Defence duties on small isolated units where there was a twenty-four hour day, seven days a week commitment which involved everyone on a basic fifty-six hour week on shift duties. Renscombe for us was a happy release to daywork only and no weekends. It meant to me the unknown pleasures of mid-morning and mid-afternoon breaks with tea and 'wads' served by a number of volunteer ladies that included the lovely married daughters of the dean living next door to the Langton camp. Flt. Lt. Griffiths one of the controllers had an insatiable interest in horse racing and had reputedly written a book on the subject. At every available opportunity he went off to attend any race meeting in the south of England to which he could find transport. I was happy to spend the evenings walking down to

Swanage, having a drink in one of the pubs and walking back again. At the weekend I enjoyed many of the lovely walks along the coastline paths in very congenial female company or made a trip to Bournemouth where one could enjoy an excellent meal of cold lobster. I was even tempted one sunny afternoon to bathe from one of the remote rocky ledges off St Albans Head.

The first principle of being a member of a small mobile signals unit was to accept that not only was everyone required to be skilled in his own trade but that he should be trained and willing to participate equally in all other aspects of mobile warfare, e.g. erection and setting to work of all signals equipment, dismantling and packing, tent pitching and striking, guard duties and defence, convoy driving and the numerous other duties required in the field. That is in addition to learning to do other people's job should they become casualties. It quickly became apparent that the low manning levels of small mobile units would ensure that under static conditions everyone would be fully occupied and when the unit was on the move everyone would be stressed to the full.

The training programme covered the assembly of radar, R/T and W/T aerials, interconnection of signals and power cables and setting the equipment to work followed by dismantling and packing; driving instruction; weapons training and fieldcraft; tent pitching and packing; medical lectures and trade training. The days began with a working parade on the square at Langton. The station warrant officer would form up the four squadrons and prove them whilst the officers walked up and down on the edge of the parade ground. The WO would then hand the parade over to me and I used to pre-position myself ready for the hand over. I do not think the WO worried about anything except his part in the parade and there was consternation one morning when I was not there having missed the last train back after an outing to Bournemouth. The WO apparently walked towards my usual position with his hand at the salute to find no one there.

The radar that we were to be allocated was very similar to the early GCI prototype except that as the result of development the one aerial now served as both transmitter and receiver and the turning gear was power driven. It was the same basic six feet cubed wooden box on a turntable mounted on a low trailer. When assembled the whole aerial was about twelve feet high and twenty-four feet across, the wooden framework on one side of the box structure was covered with fine chicken wire with dipoles mounted on it. For travelling, the end panels five feet by eight feet were removed and the upper section of the centre folded down.

The aerial trailer, the transmitter vehicle, the receiver/ops vehicle and the diesel trailer were lined up on the parade ground spaced as they would be in real operation to allow for the necessary cable and feeder runs. After some initial general instruction on the aerial assembly and cable interconnection each radar fitter, mechanic and operator was allocated a special role for his part in the aerial assembly and given more detailed instruction. After that it was just a question of practise and more practise. At the blast of a whistle a few airmen would run towards the radar aerial trailer and commence unloading the aerial framework panels whilst others would go to the transmitter vehicle and collect the wooden bracing struts, nuts and bolts, spanners, feeder wires, dipoles and feeder tensioning pulleys, mast and guys. The whole was like the traditional Royal Tournament naval gun race. Once the main wire covered frame-work panels were assembled and strengthened with their bracing struts bolted into position the sixteen pairs of half wavelength dipoles (75mm rods) and feeder wires could be attached by means of the special clamps. The feeders were connecting lengths of 3.0mm diameter copper wires held apart at about 30mm intervals by perspex spacers. The more technical members of the team had meanwhile unloaded the signal and power cables and laid them out between the vehicles and connected them. One of the signal cables was a heavy armoured coaxial 50mm in diameter running from the aerial to the receiver. The whole assembly and setting to work after a lot of practice and encouragement took only about 15 minutes.

The erection of the R/T receiver and transmitter aerials was no less impressive. From a centre point designated as the aerial position, four equally spaced distances were marked out and metal pickets driven into the ground and into the centre stabilizing plate from which the jointed lengths of the mast were assembled on the ground complete with dipoles at the top. At right angles to this was fitted a long levering arm and pulley block. Straining wires were laid out from the aerial to the picket posts. When all was ready for lifting, the long lever arm was raised to the vertical and ropes pulled steadily through the pulley block raising the main mast to the vertical where it was safely secured by the straining wires to the four pickets.

The 18kVA trailer mounted diesels were an essential part of the unit for without power nothing worked. They did not have electric start but had to be swung by means of the large starting handle and flywheel. We were to learn that starting the diesels at any hour of day or night in every

29

type of weather could be less than enjoyable, demanding physical strength and technical know-how.

Driving was an essential accomplishment for all members of the unit that could be trained, for we were to find ourselves later with a strength of about forty-five personnel and twenty-four vehicles of all shapes and sizes. Driving training was carried out on Bedford and Crossley three-tonners. I was already able to drive but changing from a passenger car to the great Crossley lorries was an adventure in itself. The steering was very heavy when carrying out slow speed manoeuvring and changing gear needed double declutching with an engine that built up its speed very slowly. I was taken to Corfe Castle on one of my few training outings and needed to change down before descending the steep winding hill. I must have left it a bit late as when I put the gear lever into neutral and my foot hard down on the accelerator I found the vehicle speed seemed to be building up faster than the engine revs and I felt things going out of control. I was extremely relieved when I felt I had enough engine revs and was able to slam the gear lever into the lower gear and concentrate on braking and steering.

The RAF Regiment instructors who taught on the use and maintenance of weapons and fieldcraft were treated as the élite at Renscombe. They lived in comparative luxury at the hutted camp at Worth, each corporal with his own room. One day we paraded at Worth for instruction in fieldcraft, which meant in general crawling through the undergrowth trying to make ourselves invisible. The heavens suddenly opened and rain descended in drops the size of mothballs. I sent the men to cover and refused point-blank to send them out to lie in the grass under such conditions. The decision came as a big shock to the RAF Regiment instructors but I heard no more of it.

The medical lectures were very popular although their emphasis was on strange diseases from the Middle East. The medical officer who gave the lectures was able to maintain the interest of everyone with a number of amusing anecdotes especially on the not so funny subject of VD. These lectures made a great impression on everyone and caused at least one of the airmen a great deal of concern before he left the UK as I shall relate later.

The time allotted to trade training was very useful. Most people knew their basic job as it related to the type of radar equipment they had previously worked on, it was just a question of some of them knuckling down under the NCOs into specialist duties with which they were unfamiliar. The crew settled down well as a unit, we were sure that we were the best and were going to give a good account of ourselves wherever we were sent. The end of the course was coming up and we did our 'Passing-out test'. This required us to drive the small convoy to a nearby site, set up the equipment and get it to work and then dismantle it and drive it back to Langton Matravers. It was just after our return that we received the unwelcome news that 'O6l was not to continue in its present form. The unit was ordered to move to Chigwell to be fitted out for special duties. The admin back up of cooks, drivers, medical orderly, clerk and so on was to be posted away and the officers replaced.

Everyone was upset as we had trained hard, learned to work together and our morale had been high. Jerry, one of the controllers spoke of a Group Captain he knew in Combined Operations Headquarters who might be able to fix things so that at least he and I could remain with 'O6l as we felt sure that our experience was as good as any other controllers that might be put in our place. Immediately after our arrival at Chigwell, Jerry and I set off for London and walked straight into Combined Ops HQ without passes and were not challenged as we searched for the Group Captain's office. It was all to no avail, the postings stood. We made our way to Verry's in Regent Street where we set about drowning our sorrows. When we came out late in the evening Jerry was a bit under the weather but I got him safely to the underground. In the crowded train a young attractive woman struck up a conversation and escorted us back to Liverpool Street station. She said she was married and working at the BBC and hinted at marital difficulties but I was hardly in the mood to be very sociable being too upset at the loss of 'O61. We got back safely to Chigwell but my time with 'O6l was ended. I would have to wait and see what my new posting would be.

Everything at Chigwell was on a massive scale of personnel, vehicles and stores. I had been allocated to No.2 Officers' Mess which was formed of dark wooden huts packed close together and I slept in a tiny spartan bedroom. This was luxury indeed compared with any of the airmen who were housed in huge aircraft hangars. Rows of double tiered bunks stretched from end to end of them and there were more than a thousand men to each hangar. Other hangars containing stores were stacked from end to end with the variety of equipment needed to keep the signals units operational in the field and specialized signals vehicles and general purpose trucks were parked nose to tail in close lines within wire compounds.

I received my new posting which was to 15054 Signals Unit also at Chigwell and about to receive its technical equipment and go out 'into the field' for its next stage of training. I at once made contact with the three other officers that had been posted to it. They were two flight lieutenant controllers and a flying officer signals officer. Both controllers were then in their early thirties, that is ten years older than myself, whilst the signals officer a Canadian was somewhat younger. Flight Lieutenant Hopper or 'Hoppy' as he was to be known to me was to be my No.1. He was tall, dark and well built. Prior to the war he had been a senior bank official in a Liverpool Street branch in London. 'Monty' Parker the other controller was an ex-regular RAF sergeant clerk who had been commissioned as a controller. He was short and swarthy with a thin black moustache. The Canadian officer 'Hank' was tall and thin and unlike so many of the Canadians I had met in the RAF he was quiet and indolent which was soon to cause trouble.

Making myself known to the airmen and NCOs I discovered that until I was posted in, unlike most units 15054 had had only an administrative officer in temporary command. This enabled the COs of other units to arrange exchanges of some of their poorer and unwanted NCOs and airmen with better ones from 15054, leaving me to take over a unit with low morale and more than the usual proportion of substandard personnel. As the unit was planned to work in forward areas next to the front line in adverse conditions, it was obvious that I had a lot of work to do to build up a unit that could fulfil such a role.

One of the most organized and busiest sections of Chigwell was the station Sick Quarters. On arrival or departure from the station everyone had to go round each of the various sections with an arrival or departure card and collect a signature from each. Entering Sick Quarters meant that one was at once ushered into one of the permanent queues for a set of inoculations. As we were to find out later anyone even if he only went in to Chigwell to collect a new vehicle had to go through the same routine. Sometimes with the aid of the injection records in one's paybook it was possible to talk one's way out of a full set of jabs but one still got one or more boosters on arrival and again on departure.

Whilst we were there we saw a vast convoy of mixed signals and general purpose vehicles in desert camouflage forming a large mobile signals unit destined for the Middle East. It was labelled with all sorts of shipping markings on the vehicle bodies and windscreens and was an impressive warlike sight as it drove out of the camp. We had a feeling that we were obviously moving towards an active involvement in the war.

Being equipped as a signals unit, even one as small as ours was a long-winded and complicated business. We were sent to the huge hangars full of stores where we checked off great piles of equipment from pages and pages of inventory that were the written quantities and variety of items considered necessary to operate in the field. The simplest section to imagine is the cookhouse with its pots and pans and cooking stoves and utensils, but each section seemed to be equally complicated or more so. Every signals vehicle had to be checked with all its aerial parts and fittings not forgetting of course each vehicle's own set of tools and paperwork. On the domestic side there were tents and tables, office equipment, forms and papers and books and the contents of our little sick quarters. The technical side had its cables and valves and components right down to acid for the unit batteries. The amount of equipment seemed to be without end. At last we seemed to have signed for everything, that is apart from our food rations, petrol and oil and our orders for deployment and training.

Our actual departure from Chigwell was an anticlimax after so much fuss. We had signed for the last vehicle, the last spare part, we had our instructions. We drove out of the camp gate on to the Chelmsford Road bound for Warbleswick near Southwold in Suffolk where we were to set up camp and start our training. We did not get more than a couple of miles or so before we had a major hiccup. One of the three-tonners stopped so the whole convoy stopped. I walked back to see one of our new three ton vehicles with a puddle of oil underneath it. Somehow one of the inexperienced Class 'B' drivers who had been trained to drive in addition to his normal signals trade had smashed the gearbox. Our MT drivers by trade arranged for the vehicle to be put on tow and off we went again.

We arrived safely at Warbleswick, put up the tents, set up the radar and were ready to carry out the training programme set by Chigwell. Each day's programme was scheduled to start at 06.30 with an hour's physical training. I thought this was unreasonable and explained to the men on parade that I would be happy with half an hour of PT starting at 07.00 and that the Duty Corporal for the day would be in charge and responsible for seeing that the training was carried out. I awoke next morning and left my tent shortly after 07.00 to see how things were going. Nothing seemed to be stirring on the camp until I saw a lone figure in vest and shorts dispiritedly moving slowly between the tents. It was the Duty Corporal who was apparently making little progress in getting the men out of bed, let alone leading their PT session. I then made my decision, it seemed that if discipline was to be imposed then it had to be done by me leading from the front. From then on I led the men on their morning PT and we started with good early morning runs down the road before breakfast.

The training programme was much the same as that carried out at Renscombe but I had to start again with a crew that had many obvious weaknesses. We practised putting the aerials up several times a day using a stopwatch to measure progress and each time trying to improve the technique. Driving instruction went on continuously in an attempt to qualify everyone either on the four wheeled vehicles or on the motor cycles that were used for convoy escort or for message work. The three little BSA 250cc motor cycles with which we were issued were very pleasant to ride but were not designed to survive wartime conditions. After the first hundred miles the soft metal of the toolbox fastenings had given way and the tools were lost. We trained on common land but this caused handlebars and main frames to crack.

It was essential to get as many men as possible qualified to drive the vehicles as our establishment was only three drivers by trade, just enough to drive the vehicles with trailers. Training of drivers was not easy as the Crossley vehicles were large and heavy to handle and very frightening to many of the trainee drivers. Driving with the vehicles in convoy formed a great part of the driving practice for the 'B' Class drivers and was a hair-raising experience for all involved.

We practised our first unit move by packing everything, the signals equipment, the domestic tentage, personal belongings and then driving around the county and coming back to the same site to the great surprise of most as was intended. This got everyone used to packing his own belongings, the tent which he shared with seven others and the cook-house equipment, the medical section, headquarters tent, MT and latrines as well as yet again dismantling the radar and communications equipment. Toughening up by route marches was even more unpopular than PT, presumably because it was of longer duration. We tried a move to another site setting up the domestic camp in a coniferous wood which we found had considerable disadvantages, not the least that it made everything so dirty from the fine black dusty earth.

As might be expected there were few recreational facilities. We went up to the nearby RAF radar station at Darsham and spent an evening or two chatting with the few officers there whilst our airmen made contact with the WAAFs or else made for the nearest pub which was some distance away. Monty Parker one of the two flight lieutenant controllers was the best organized as the result of the following incident.

Whilst we were at Chigwell there had been a couple of mystery telephone calls for me from a woman caller. I was very puzzled that there should be such a call for me as I had given no one my telephone number and all military numbers in wartime were withheld from the public. Monty was surprised at my lack of interest and asked if he could take the next call. It turned out to be the woman from the BBC who had somehow through her job managed to get the camp number. Following the call Monty was swamped with regular little postal gifts and invited off to free weekends of loving entertainment about which we received a blow by blow account. Monty was of course delighted and I felt at times a little regretful as life was a little lonely as the CO of a small unit camping in the wilds of Suffolk.

We met up with another small signals unit that was camping near by also out from Chigwell and under for training. It was an even smaller unit than ours with only one officer. He was no engineer and was faced with the problem of erecting for the first time without any formal instruction a large wooden tower from a great pile of wooden slats and a few assembly drawings. Whilst I would have liked to have helped and to have the satisfaction of building the tower myself I had enough problems of my own. We wished him luck and left him alone to work out his own solution.

As was to be expected we were to have personnel troubles within the unit. Hank the signals officer was very reluctant to leave his bed in the morning and had almost literally to be forced out of it. He was a poor example to his section and decidedly lacking in the leadership I required from this most important section of the unit. Then there was the little cockney MT corporal who considered his responsibilities and authority to be greater than mine. He would come up to me waving a hand in a vague sort of salute and putting his head on one side would repeat, "I carn 'ave it, Sir, I carn 'ave it." I am afraid I did the situation little good by asking "And what can't you have, Corporal?" It appeared the trouble was usually that Hoppy or I had used a vehicle without his express permission.

Our cook Corporal Gallop who was later to be such an asset to the unit found the going very hard in those early days. It was a great shock for any cook to be posted from a permanent station to a mobile signals unit with its primitive cooking conditions, irregular mealtimes and constant upheaval of moving. Later on we could rely on Corporal Gallop to produce hot meals within minutes at any time or any place and it was on this that much of the good morale of the unit was to be based.

The NCOs of the unit generally lacked self-assertiveness and experience but with my urging and backing things steadily got better. My main worry was the technical section comprising the radar fitters and mechanics. I could train the radar operators myself but I needed a good technical section to get the best performance out of the radar and to keep it operational. Our Technical Officer was of little help in improving a weak area.

We received orders to move to the permanent GCI at Trimley Heath for two weeks training with live aircraft. We set up the convoy near by and the technical staff kept it in running order whilst the controllers and radar operators worked in the operations room of the static station. We controllers were happy to carry out practice interceptions once again with night fighters whilst the unit magazine later recorded that 'The operators were more than satisfied to work on the static station gear with refreshments served at regular intervals by radar type WAAFs.'

It was mid-August when we received orders to return to Chigwell. Only a few days before Hank the signals officer had had a nasty accident on one of the motor cycles. A large lorry and trailer turned right in front of him and he was trapped between the lorry and trailer. He was fortunate

36

to escape serious injury although the whole of his arm, body and leg on the one side was a horrible purple pulp. Making our usual arrival call on the Sick Quarters when we arrived at Chigwell I took the Senior Medical Officer aside and told him of Hank's injuries and expressed my opinion that he would be better off without the usual jabs. "Nonsense," said the Canadian SMO, "we Canadians can take it." He then gave the jabs to Hank who later that same evening collapsed and was taken to hospital where he was detained for a couple of weeks.

The unit received a certain amount of re-equipment at Chigwell before being posted as a unit to Blue Forces the mobile airfield Group that was to form a major part of the air assault forces for the Second Front. Our parent unit was to be the 83 Group Control Centre which was responsible for the planning and direction of the fighters and fighter bombers of the Group. We, that is 15054 with two other similar units Nos, 15053 and 8007, were to provide the air picture and radar control facilities. Whilst at Chigwell I gave a pep talk to the unit outlining the important and leading part I expected the unit to play in the invasion of Europe. It was a most successful talk since it resulted in a number of the less enthusiastic members of the unit reporting sick and being posted away. I shed no tears over the departure of the troublesome MT corporal who took great pains to get an interview with me to tell me how much he regretted being unable to stay with the unit because of his stomach troubles.

We were no longer 15054 Signals Unit. With our move came a change of title, we were now to be known by our operational role that of Forward Director Post. This was immediately abbreviated to 15054 FDP or even '054 which was invariably used by everyone from then on. In a very short while the actual meaning of the letters was forgotten.

Our first site with Blue Group was at an old GCI site at Willesborough just outside Ashford in Kent. I reported in to the Group Control Centre which was a mobile version of a Sector Operations Centre with a large General Situation Map (GSM) on a horizontal table on which the positions and direction of aircraft in the area were marked with arrows alongside which were plaques showing the number of aircraft, the height and the raid number and identification. There were the usual facilities for radio communication with the aircraft and direction finding on the fighters by taking bearings on the aircraft radio transmissions. Planning duties by officers tasking the squadrons were carried out in a cabin overlooking the GSM.

I discussed with the Chief Controller the unit role and it was arranged that 15054's plots on the air situation would be passed to the GCC and displayed on the GSM. This supply of our air information either by landline or W/T to the GCC gave a new realism to our training.

We set up the domestic camp in a field across the road from the technical vehicles. A small stream ran through the field and by building a small dam across the lads made a fine bathing pool. This provided a great deal of enjoyment until one day someone found a dead sheep in it. The popularity of bathing declined rapidly in favour of football.

The toughening up continued. We were no longer ordinary 'Boys in Blue' or 'Brylcreem Boys', we all wore khaki battledress, heavy army marching boots and gaiters with our ordinary blue RAF caps and badges. We had also been issued with brown leather sleeveless jerkins that were to be a great comfort when the cold weather came. The morale of the unit was rising fast and the men took a pride in being different and began to think of themselves as members of a small élite. The training was not without pain however. I took the unit on a route march with full kit and each man was issued with a small amount of raw meat and vegetables. The distance was only about ten miles but the day turned out to be the hottest of the year. Each man having to cook his own meal over an open fire hardly made me more popular and everyone arrived back exhausted and most in ill-humour. I think that half the unit reported sick the next day with blisters, aches and pains. The unit was never to reach the high standards of marching and singing associated with the German army.

I was called to the GCC one day and taken into the Group Captain who chatted generally about the unit activities and expressed his pleasure at the way in which the training was going. He said that he would like us one day to carry out a night move and when I enquired when he had in mind he said, "I think tonight would be as good a time as any, don't you?" to which I had no ready answer. I had a quick look around for a site and found a good one at Swingfield at the back of Folkestone and on my return to the unit put a restriction on anyone going out that night.

As soon as it was really dark I blew my whistle and announced the move. It could not have come at a more awkward time as we had taken a great deal of trouble to camouflage both the technical convoy and the domestic site using the usual camouflage netting supported by special frameworks and a covering of brushwood. Despite all of that and the fact that it was our first night move we got on the road in remarkably good time. We drove to Swingfield and in the darkness with the aid of a few hurricane lamps set up the radar convoy and got it operational and then erected the minimum number of tents so that those not on duty could get some sleep. It was a tiring business as everyone had been awake all day but it was good practice for what was to come after we landed in France.

Towards the end of the setting up of the tents it was discovered that one of the MT drivers was missing. He was found at last fast asleep in his vehicle. The man was a professional scrounger and had been up on several charges of breach of discipline. I had at that time the enormous powers of a detachment commander, that is I could give up to twenty-eight days detention (imprisonment) as punishment although I never in fact gave detention to anyone as it was impracticable to lose a man's services from a small mobile unit. Other forms of punishment were far better as there were always lots of fatigues and guard duties to be done. I worked instead on getting rid of the man, who was unpopular with everyone, by encouraging him to apply for a voluntary exchange with a driver from another unit.

In due course an exchange of drivers was arranged but when I looked at the service record of the newcomer I was startled to find that he had been given detention at some time for urinating on his corporal's bed! However it was an excellent swap as we acquired someone who was capable, always willing, versatile and polite, a real asset to the unit. We heard later that our departing driver on arrival at his new unit had asked rashly if anyone in his billet wanted a fight. Someone did and broke his arm! As soon as the man recovered from this he drove a new vehicle straight into a lamppost.

The unit had an intense rivalry with 15053 our sister unit. Millbank, its CO, told me that at one time that he had moved so often that his airmen coming back from leave had a job to locate their unit and spent days travelling around south-east England looking for it. Millbank was very keen on fishing and managed to find several sites where he could fish whilst sitting outside his tent. He had a senior Flight Lieutenant named Pattison who as a civilian had had some contact with the Navy. He used his knowledge to draw 50 fine duffle coats from Navy stores for the airmen of 15053 and the coats were a great source of envy to us. No. 8007 which was the other FDP unit was considered weaker opposition. It had suffered two major calamities, the first was when they had disguised their convoy of technical vehicles as a line of straw stacks. The camouflage was excellent but a spark from one of the diesels set a number of the radar vehicles alight and one of the controllers lost his uniform jacket and his money in the blaze. As if this was not enough they had driven one of their outsize signal vehicles under a low railway bridge which had removed a large part of the body and aerial framework.

Swingfield was a popular site. There was a good pub not far away and the discovery of large numbers of horse mushrooms some as big as a dinner plate made life under canvas very enjoyable despite the many chores. Among the minor difficulties was when one of the airmen married and brought his new and attractive wife down to stay in accommodation near by. She tended to haunt the site boundary causing an unwanted diversion from the daily tasks. I took her with me one day when I had to make a routine trip to the GCC thinking that it would make a pleasant break for her to see the country around and also get her away from the camp for a while. It was pointed out that my innocent gesture could be given a wrong interpretation and I was very pleased when the newlywed's holiday was over and she returned home.

All units were called to take part in a full scale invasion exercise. Our unit joined with the GCC making an enormous convoy of 400 vehicles that set off towards Portsmouth where we were scheduled to embark on landing craft. A small convoy of vehicles is difficult to control and 400 was nothing more than a disaster. Perhaps the leading vehicle did travel at a regular slow speed but for everyone else it was a series of long waits followed by the vehicle in front starting up and then disappearing at high speed. After getting one's vehicle going and doing a high speed chase after the vehicle in front one seemed almost invariably to find it stationary just around the next blind bend. The system of moving towards the embarkation point at that time was for the units to move from one transit camp to another sleeping in the permanent tents and bedding and messing in the communal messes provided. At the first of these camps the lads took the opportunity of fixing name boards they had painted to the front of the jeeps of the three FDP units which were normally driven by their COs. Mine read 'Kemp's Circus', 15053 read 'Millbank's Wanderers', and that of 8007. 'The Fire Raisers'. The name boards were to survive for a long time.

After passing through various transit camps on our way to the embarkation point we finally reached Waterlooville just outside Portsmouth and parked on the roadside with a vast number of other vehicles awaiting further orders. There had been rumours floating around but when our orders came they were unexpected. Due to bad weather the exercise had been cancelled and all units were to travel independently to Middle Wallop on Salisbury Plain. Knowing that we were probably the most mobile unit I blew my whistle which was an essential item in our moves, ordered the drivers into their vehicles and got our convoy on the road before anyone else.

Driving in wartime with a convoy of outsize vehicles was not easy. Most signposts had been removed and if one led the convoy at night one had to grope along peering into the blackness with little help from the vehicle headlamps that were blacked out except for narrow slits in the metal covering over the glass. For the drivers following it meant staring hard ahead and concentrating on the differential hub of the vehicle in front that was painted white and lit by a small wattage bulb.

It had been dark for some time when I found myself leading the unit convoy in the middle of nowhere knowing that Middle Wallop could not be far away but not having any idea of the route for the last few miles. I had realized that I was now also leading a long convoy of other vehicles that stretched for miles behind me. Suddenly I noticed approaching from my right yet another long line of vehicles stretching back over a hill. I increased my speed a little and we reached the junction almost together but I was just sufficiently ahead to prevent the other convoy turning on to the road ahead of me. I enquired from the leading driver of the line of vehicles where he was going and received the answer "Middle Wallop." I made the obvious reply, "So are we," and as there was only one other way to go I drove straight on to find the station within a few miles. As we entered the camp and identified ourselves to the guards we were directed to a hangar where we could sleep the night with the warning, "There is only a small amount of straw available to sleep on and 1,000 men are expected in tonight."

Conditions may not have been comfortable but it was an achievement to have found Middle Wallop at all on such a dark night. In the morning our unit cooks being well trained by now served up a good hot breakfast which was more than most of the other units enjoyed. An even greater pleasure was to secure our release from the Exercise and to move back to Swingfield and set up the radar and domestic site again. Winter however was setting in and life under canvas was no longer so pleasant. There was talk of winter quarters and we were pleased when orders came for us to move into the RAF station at Lympne. There were fighter bomber squadrons on the airfield and we watched them on the radar as they took off to attack the V1 sites across the Channel. Unfortunately we had no operational role as the air surveillance was carried out by the static UK radars.

It was a pleasant change for me to live in an officers' mess and to mix once again with aircrew. One of the squadrons was a Dutch fighter squadron and all the pilots spoke excellent English. They were however very keen to improve their mastery of colloquial English and RAF phraseology and if one of them picked up a new expression he took it back to his crew room and they all practised it and trotted it out on every possible occasion. I well remember watching a game of snooker when someone made a fluke shot and his opponent said a rough equivalent of, "If he fell in the cess-pit he would come out smelling of roses." The next day one heard the expression being used all the time.

I took the opportunity to visit the new radar (Type 16) at Hythe which was used for controlling the long range fighter sweeps and daylight bomber strikes over France. The radar presentation for the controller was a large horizontal PPI display on which the radar trace rotated and the fine narrow beam echoes showed up on it. The controller thus had all the advantages of immediate radar responses in large map form but could also mark in chinagraph pencil the tracks with identification and heights. I noted that all the WAAF posted to the station seemed to be above average for looks and wondered if this was specially arranged to increase fighter pilots' interest in radar control.

The FDP units were directed to take part in 'Exercise Fordirect'. This was said to have as its object the investigation of the feasibility of ground controllers working on their radar directing the fighter bombers into visual range of their targets. There were many in authority however who saw the coming of the Second Front as an even more glorious 'free for all' opportunity for pilots to attack enemy motor transports and war material than that of North Africa. They saw no requirement for interference by ground controllers and did not intend to have any. The exercise was not therefore carried out using the narrow beam width low coverage radar referred to as the Type 14 but by using the Type 15 of the FDPs. The Type 14 had a beam width of only one degree, the Type 15 some eighteen degrees. The Type 14 was available in mobile form and was issued to 85 Group radar units. It was so good that in a re-engineered form was to be issued to UK coastal radars ten years later.

We directed photographic aircraft over designated pin-points and told them when to take their vertical photographs. The results were never made available to the FDP COs and we were never invited to a debrief to express our views. The veterans of the Eighth Army and those of the Desert Air Force were to find the conditions in Europe vastly different from those in the desert. It is said that the army took a long while to adapt to them, 83 Group never did. Had a different attitude been taken to ground control I am convinced far better targeting and far less pilot casualties would have resulted.

I was making one of my routine calls to the GCC when in the course of conversation I was asked if I knew that I was off to Troon in Scotland the next day for a two week course in Combined Operations? I admitted my ignorance and found to my astonishment that it applied in fact to the whole unit. We packed up the convoy, tentage and personal kit yet again and left it in the care of another FDP No.8024 and went off by train.

At Troon personnel of all three services were given instruction in seaborne assault operations and working of Combined Operations. To help with inter-service understanding the working parade each day was taken by an officer of the Navy, Army and RAF in rotation. The most instructive part of the course was learning to load and off-load from landing craft. Loading an LCT (Landing Craft Tank) so that its vehicles could run straight down the ramp on to the enemy beach could only be done by reversing the vehicles one by one up the steep ramp on to the boat. Nearly all of us were Class 'B' drivers, that is not drivers by trade but had been taught to drive in order to operate as drivers during all unit moves and frequently for sick runs, ration runs, water runs and so on. However, we did not have the experience of the regular MT drivers and practising reversing with a large loaded vehicle up very steep ramps was an exciting and sometimes frightening business. To assist the driver another man acted as mate. He stood in front of the vehicle and by raising one arm or the other indicated to the driver that he should apply left or right hand down, or stop as required. The vehicle often did not make the fairly narrow opening on to the landing craft and in a moment of doubt or panic drivers often put out the clutch so that the vehicle came roaring down the slope out of control. We were fortunate I thought not to have any casualties.

A less enjoyable feature of Troon for many was the assault course. This took its toll on the overweight and the over forties of which we fortunately had few. The morale of the unit by now was such that those more fortunate helped the others over. Corporal Banham writing in the 15054 unit magazine recorded,'. . . at Troon where personnel are taught to be Commandos in not more than six lessons. I myself dare not shoot a line about this course as doubtless many readers will recall the fact that I had to be hauled over various obstacles on the assault course.'

Fortunately the RAF was not involved in a Navy training exercise I saw for the first time there. By the side of the parade ground was a section of high wall that had large holes built into it about two feet above the ground. Ratings in working undress were engaged in shovelling great heaps of coal through the holes. I assumed that when all the coal was on the other side they then shovelled it back again.

We were detailed for instruction periods at regular times but the instructors had a habit of turning up late. Rather than have the men standing around for long periods in the cold, I used to wait until the instructors were ten minutes overdue and then dismiss the men ordering them to turn up again in time for the next period. On completion of the course we were all entitled to wear the coveted Combined Operations badge on our uniforms.

We returned to Lympne, collected our vehicles and set up the convoy once again. By now we had moved twenty-four times and were well and truly mobile. We could dismantle the radar and communications aerials, disconnect the cables and pack them, pack one's own personal kit, strike the tent and all the other domestic tents, load up the food, fuel, equipment and belongings and fill up the various waste pits, line up all the vehicles in convoy order and still be on the road in an hour and a half.

The year (1943) was coming to an end but we still had two moves to make. We were ordered off to the Christchurch area for two weeks of training at RAF Sopley one of the permanent GCIs. It was two weeks before Christmas and bitterly cold and damp. To keep off the worst of the weather we set up the tents inside a temporary hangar on an unoccupied reserve airfield but it seemed to make little difference to the cold. However, we all enjoyed the experience of working a watch system once again in the permanent operations block which meant that the lads were able to enjoy coveted twenty-four hour passes.

On Christmas Eve we made a very fast convoy run all the way back to Kent where we had been ordered into accommodation at RAF Hawkinge near Folkestone. There was just time to send half the unit off on Christmas leave and arrange for the others to go off for the New Year on their return.

We spent three long weary months at Hawkinge. Accommodation was crowded and the officers slept on camp beds in the old billiard room. Even so that was better than being under canvas at that time of the year. I had caught a bad dose of flu when home on leave and had been dosed with the new sulphur drugs. They may have cured the flu but they left me as weak as a rat for weeks afterwards. I used to crawl around looking at the lads for a short while and then I had to go and rest. With the convoy packed and the weather bad there was little to do but paint the vehicles yet again with the latest camouflage colours and designs sent by the experts, service the tents with water repellent, paint more unit signs, carry out trade training and generally try and keep people occupied. There were operational fighter squadrons on the station and the aircraft flew off regularly on their missions but we were not part of their life and had no knowledge of their day to day work.

Our khaki battledress was withdrawn and we became once again boys in blue just like all the other RAF personnel on the station. The lads enjoyed all the advantages of static life on a permanent station. They had the regular morning and afternoon NAAFI break with a cup of char and a wad, no night duties, few guards, regular leave, almost every evening out and of course they enjoyed the station dances with the WAAFs in attendance. In the officers' mess there was a wonderful party with enormous quantities of excellent food that made a harsh contrast to the wartime rations. Even so it was depressing waiting for the spring and the expected Second Front.

Being so close to Folkestone meant that the area was within range of the German coastal guns that fired now and again. I had gone down one day to the outskirts of the town to visit the CO of a small unit somewhat similar to ourselves who was living in a small wooden hut. He was over fifty years old but had somehow managed to complete no less than three Combined Operations courses at Troon! He was lying on his bed talking to me when the shelling warning was given. He did no more than reach under his bed for his tin helmet which he placed over his testicles and carried on talking.

Towards the end of March to the relief of all we were once again mobile and took up our duties as an FDP again, setting up our radar here and there in the SE counties and telling the picture to the GCC. We moved off west to the Horsham and Lewes areas and stopped off for a night at Worthing. It coincided with a night bombing raid by the Germans which the local GCI tried to intercept without success. The reason they gave for failure was interference on their radar picture which they blamed on to us, although our radar was not switched on at the time. The next day we received some very rude verbal messages and signals from the GCC and Group Headquarters telling us to move off elsewhere.

Changes were being made to our equipment. When we first left Chigwell we had a number of trailers which included the diesel generators and the Type 15 Aerial. We also had some poorly designed R/T and W/T vehicles. All this was changing. The Type 15 aerial was now a prime mover on a smart six wheeled Austin chassis, a new and smaller transmitter was fitted inside the aerial cabin and the large armoured coaxial cable was no longer required. The radar aerial itself now had an extra box section at the top which was the new IFF facility allowing friendly aircraft to identify themselves. The diesels were each on the same smart six wheeled chassis as were the R/T section vehicles. Some of the Crossley GP vehicles had been replaced by the easier to drive Bedfords and the water bowser trailer was replaced by a small tanker. The convoy was beginning to look quite smart.

The most important change was the issue of an additional search radar that came with aerial, receiver vehicle (normally known as the operations or 'Ops') and another diesel. The new radar was called a Type 11 and operated on 25cms wavelength the same as that of the German radars. The aerial was parabolic in shape and extremely easy to erect as the two end sections just swung out and were bolted into position. It had a much narrower beamwidth than the old Type 15 which made the PPI picture much clearer. It generally had a longer aircraft detection range but the vertical coverage was not so good causing aircraft tracks to disappear for several sweeps of the aerial.

With the increase in radar equipment came an increase in personnel and I am pleased to say that we were very fortunate in getting a number of good airmen and NCOs. The unit by now was very experienced and its morale was high, newcomers settled in quickly and helped raise the standard still further. The number of new vehicles increased once again

47

our need to train new 'B' Class drivers.

We settled in to our mobile routine again spending a few days here and there evaluating the radar performance on different types of terrain and testing the ranges of our wireless communications. It was the responsibility of the Army Air Formation Signals units to provide land-lines between the GCC and the airfields and the radar units. It always seemed that they were not only able to locate us on each new site from a map reference in a very short space of time but were able to provide and maintain telephone lines in working order with remarkable efficiency.

At each move the gridded maps over the PPIs had to be redrawn to take into account the new location pin-point which was always at the centre of the PPI. The Type 11 vertical coverage pattern also had to be drawn for the site slope because it was from this that we could provide a height approximation on the aircraft we picked up. Now that we had two plan position radars it was necessary to co-ordinate the information from them before passing the information to the GCC. We therefore opened up the side panels of the Type 15 receiver vehicle and backed the Type 11 receiver vehicle on to it making a fairly large operations room and built our own map board on the wall under a perspex cover on which we could mark our aircraft tracks.

Striking camp every three or four days, packing, unpacking, driving and carrying out normal duties did not leave much time or opportunity for social activities other than an occasional beer. I did take the opportunity to visit the magnificent home of an old colleague Robin McCall in the Winchester area. He was to land successfully in Normandy only 30 minutes after the initial landings and set up the wire and canvas and cardboard vehicles of his convoy in front of a line of tanks which hull down were acting as artillery.

I was detailed for a short exercise in Studland Bay near Swanage where the Canadian 2nd Division was to carry out a landing exercise. I had a chance to drive a White half-track scout car around the narrow lanes of Hampshire and to renew for a brief moment a very happy acquaintanceship at Langton Matravers. After spending an uncomfortable night in a vehicle high above Studland the support aircraft did not materialize due to early morning fog on the airfields. At the exercise debriefing inter-service co-operation was not helped by the Army remark of "No RAF air support as usual."

On my way back to the unit I made contact with Mickey Lovell who was at Middle Wallop. He had been a Sector Controller at Fairwood

Common near Swansea when I was at the GCI at Ripperston. He invited me to meet him at 'The Mucky Duck' pub and I spent hours driving around the countryside in the blackout before I finally found myself at 'The Black Swan' which was its correct name. It was then well past closing time but the bar was open until long after midnight for a few favoured friends.

Some decades later I was driving in the area and related the story to my passengers. We stopped and asked our way to The Black Swan and were assured that there was no pub of that name in the area and I was accused of making up the story. On going into another pub for a drink I made further enquiry and was told, "Oh yes, but its usual name around here is The Mucky Duck."

It was at the end of April that the unit suffered its first casualty. We were camped close to Alton when our disciplinary Corporal Clark did not return from a duty run on one of the motor cycles and he was later reported by the police to have died as the result of an accident. No other vehicle was involved nor was there any evidence of speeding. It seems that he hit a patch of gravel on a bend and skidded into a ditch and hit a tree. He was one of our most reliable junior NCOs and his loss was much regretted. It appeared that he was having domestic trouble at the time and one wondered if he had lost his concentration as a result since he was a competent driver.

There was a big and marked change for the better when after much campaigning on my part Hank our Canadian signals officer was replaced by another Canadian Bill Jones. No two men could have been more different. Our new officer was large, pleasant and easygoing but keen on his work and always ready to join in and set an example. We were also strengthened on the administrative side acquiring Flying Officer Taylor as adjutant and Sergeant Poulter as the sergeant disciplinarian. Both were older than most of us and they applied great seriousness to running the administrative and domestic arrangement of the unit. Because of the constant mobility these were heavy tasks. Sergeant Poulter was a small quiet rugged man who earned the respect of all by his quiet dogged persistence in getting things done. The unit was generally known as Kemp's Circus but those involved in running the various domestic activities either by trade or when co-opted were known as Jim Poulter's Army.

Morale in most of the small units was very high. The men revelled in being different, in wearing marching boots and gaiters and the sleeveless leather jerkins that were such a comfort and convenience. They were proud to have completed the Combined Operations course and to be entitled to wear the coveted Combined Operations badge with its Commando implications. However, the personnel of the larger units had not been so trained and could not wear the badge. The result was an order issued by 83 Group Headquarters forbidding all personnel to wear the badge. It did nothing to improve morale.

We moved back to the old site at Ashford in Kent where the farmer tried his hardest to dissuade us from going into the field we had used as our domestic site on the previous occasion. He shed tears explaining how we would upset his ewes and newly-born lambs. We felt less sympathetic when a little later we saw him castrating the young lambs and tossing the bits to his dog. It was noticeable how Southern England was filling up with vast numbers of troops, with tanks and guns parked in unending lines along the sides of the wider roads such as the Hog's Back near Guildford. It was obvious to all that the time of the Second Front was getting near.

We moved back again to an elevated site near Alton. The unit was running well, every man knew his job and many of them could claim a good knowledge of other trades. It was no trouble for the operators to lay and connect up telephone lines either within the ops rooms (we now had two) or out to the domestic site. Almost everyone could drive either the large vehicles or the smaller ones or at least a motor cycle, although I was of the opinion that it took a great deal of riding skill to marshal the convoy with the motor cycles. After directing the convoy at a road junction it was then necessary for the motor cyclist to overtake the whole convoy which was no easy task on the narrow roads as they were then. The motor cycles we had were in constant use either for running messages or for convoy escort. We had started with the BSA 250cc machines but these did not stand up long to the hard wear. Then we had Matchless and then the Harley-Davidson 750cc machines. I took advantage of a training run on one of the new Harley-Davidsons to call in at my home in Weybridge. I found on checking that the machine was using petrol at an alarming rate and stopped at an Army unit to refuel. The unit was not very helpful and it took ages to find someone to issue petrol. When I went to start the machine it would not fire. It was a very hot day and I kicked and pushed the machine until I was exhausted. Finally I realized that unlike the British bikes at that time the Harley had an ignition switch and I had failed to switch on. The bikes were very comfortable to ride but I felt the handlebars were rather too wide for convoy work on our narrow roads.

During wartime plain language was not allowed for messages sent by W/T and all of ours were coded by means of a small American coding machine called an M209 which was also used in the American bombers. After setting a daily code on a set of master wheels the message was coded by means of feeding in the letters and rotating the wheels. Suddenly two cipher sergeants were posted to the unit and arrived with their own vehicle together with higher grading coding systems. Like most of the changes to the unit they came to us entirely without warning.

Our last operational site was to be at Emsworth near Havant just north of the A27. It was a small field at the end of a quiet street with a short row of houses. We set up the radar and went on with our final preparations. Unexpectedly we were allocated a new specialist height finding radar. It was known as a Type 13 but the aerial was generally referred to as 'the Nodding Horror' or more usually 'the Cheese'. The radar aerial came on the now standard six wheeled chassis on which was mounted a turntable and transmitter cabin. A very large hollow steel section rather like a crescent moon pivoted at its centre, was mounted on a steel framework built out from the top of the cabin. When in operation it nodded, constantly sweeping the sky in a narrow vertical plane. The aerial could be rotated from within the operations room to face the direction of the aircraft whose height was required. Presentation was on a cathode ray tube where a bright line pivoted at the bottom left hand corner swept up and down. The aircraft response showed as a small vertical line at its range from the station measured from the left hand corner pivot. This response left an afterglow and a height could be read from its position on a series of horizontal lines drawn on the display. When two aircraft were more or less on the same bearing the position of one above or below the other could be seen immediately. Later we were to see bombs leaving aircraft in the same way.

The radar fitters were at once very busy doing the final connections and adjustments to the new equipment and mounting the display in the Type 11 Ops room. The operators were busy mastering the assembly and dismantling of the aerial until it could be done in a matter of minutes. The cheese section when we were on the move was fixed lengthways on the vehicle alongside its turning cabin. To erect the aerial the cheese was first lowered to the ground by rotation about a horizontal lengthwise hinge. When on the ground the hinge-pin was removed and the cheese manhandled around so that its open face was on the ground and lying at right angles to the vehicle. The end nearest the vehicle was then lifted by hand and a hinge-pin inserted across the end. A steel mounting frame was assembled and bolted on to the top edge of the transmitter cabin and the cheese then winched up into position and fitted on to its pivot on the mounting frame. The hinge-pin was removed and the cheese finally connected to the nodding mechanism.

We felt that we were now just about ready to go to war, fully equipped and well trained. Our Air Officer Commanding made his first and only inspection of the unit. We showed him all over the equipment and at the end he gave me his final words of encouragement. "Very nice, Kemp," he said, and then smiling he continued, "but if I were you I would put a little black boy up there to tell you when the enemy is coming," and he pointed to the roof of the tall transmitter vehicle. I did not pass on his last remark to the lads. It was a well-known fact that the AOC had no time for radar or any form of ground control of his aircraft and that his call was, "Just give me more aircraft and I will be satisfied."

We received orders to pack the convoy; a photographer arrived to take pictures of each one of us for the new identity cards that were to be issued; the MT section went off for instruction on vehicle waterproofing and came back with a vast amount of pieces of iron pipe, waterproof canvas and large tubes of Bostick. All vehicles were to be fitted with breather tubes and waterproofing that would enable them to run for a short time in water up to six feet deep. However, this waterproofing could only be done in stages but the initial stages were put in hand right away on all vehicles.

I gave the unit a pep talk and told them all of the importance of the work we were going to do and that we would be landed early into the beach-head. I had a nasty shock when a few days later I received a letter that had been opened by the censor. It had been written by one of the new cipher sergeants and repeated word for word the timing of our landing that I had given in my talk. This was a dreadful shock as everyone of us working on radar had been well trained in security matters. It was my impression that cipher personnel would have been equally well trained.

Any breach of security calls for investigation and a serious one such as had been reported occurring just before the invasion could have threatened the lives of thousands. It was fortunate that my remarks contained no firm invasion date but gave our landing time as the number of days after D-Day. I had no idea myself of when D-Day would be, it was a well kept secret. The sergeant was charged with a breach of censorship and released whilst I sent on details of the affair to Group and waited for their orders to take a Summary of Evidence prior to a court martial.

Everyone was now issued with a khaki battledress in exchange for one of the blues. The intention was that khaki should be worn when we were anywhere near the front line so that we did not get confused with that of the German army. It was a wise precaution but the timing of the instruction of when to wear blue or khaki was often not well thought out. If the front was static for a time then the order came out to wear blue, but this was then usually the time 15054 was rushing forward again. We had worn khaki when the unit was first formed but it had been withdrawn when we went into winter quarters.

I was informed that the early shipping space allocated to the unit would be limited and I was left to decide what radar I would take on the main or early party. I chose to take the Type 11 and 13 for a variety of operational reasons, leaving the Type 15 aerial, transmitter vehicle, a diesel and a three-tonner with one corporal and sufficient airmen to drive the vehicles to follow later as more shipping space became available. I did not realize then, that leaving these men static for a few weeks within easy reach of the social temptations of Emsworth would cause trouble which I was not to hear of until we had been in France for some time.

With the convoy packed and leave cancelled there was little to do and it seemed that it would be necessary once more to start route marches to keep the lads fit and occupied. However this was not to be as we suddenly received orders for our main party to move immediately to our concentration area at Old Sarum near Salisbury.

We arrived at Old Sarum in fine weather as one would expect in early June, reception staff showed us where to park our vehicles and where we were to sleep. We made contact with several other units and exchanged news with people we knew. During the night we were woken by a great noise of aircraft flying low overhead and got out of bed and went outside to see vast numbers of aircraft all with their navigation lights on at low level heading in the same direction. We surmised quite rightly that the invasion was under way. The actual date was a surprise to all of us as the secret had been well kept. The next day we were called to the first of many briefings. At the briefing we were given a general outline of the invasion area, the beaches and the forces that were involved. We were again warned of the need for good security and given a list of the other briefings we were to receive. These involved the shipping allocation, rations, routes and timings on our way to the dock. On the operations side we were to be given our operational site location, a large quantity of maps, recognition signals and codes and frequencies for R/T and W/T.

Our shipping allocation was most satisfactory. Although the unit was to be split up over three landing vessels we were to have all the signals vehicles and my jeep on one LCT (Landing Craft Tank) TT207. The domestic vehicles were to travel on a landing ship LST TT1022 with forward elements of the GCC, whilst the water bowser was all alone on LCT TT208. That meant that if the LCT TT207 got ashore OK we were in business. A minor worry was that another unit might appropriate our unaccompanied bowser. The shipping allocation meant that we could get on with the movement order for personnel allocation to the vehicles and the numbering of vehicles. Each vehicle carried its shipping code, the loading number and number in its driving convoy. Any spare personnel were occupied in carrying out the next stage of waterproofing.

When we had the details of frequencies we were able to brief the R/T, W/T and Ops Sections and with our proposed site pin-pointed we could draw the PPI grids in advance of our setting up in France. We all received our new 1250s or identity cards which for the first time carried a photograph of the holder. I was very impressed with the number of my card as it seemed so small starting with a series of noughts.

Since last year when we were on an invasion exercise the embarkation system had been simplified. Instead of passing from one transit camp to another steadily working towards the docks we now assembled in the one concentration area for briefings and then drove to an embarkation area from which we were to be called forward for actual onloading on to our landing craft.

The situation on the 7th June (D-Day plus one) was that we were due for a briefing at 18.00 to receive details of our next move forward. This was delayed for an hour and when we were briefed at last, it was to hear that we were to move at 10.30 and 12.30 the next day, the signals vehicles to be the first away. Once more giving the vehicles a final check it was found that the GP Crossley that carried all the technical spares had a faulty valve, this was a common complaint that subsequently put thousands of Army vehicles off the road during the campaign. We were immediately allocated another vehicle from reserve but everything from the unserviceable vehicle had to be unloaded and reloaded and the new vehicle waterproofed and marked with its shipping and convoy numbers. It was getting on for midnight before the task was completed.

The next morning we were up and prepared for the 'off', the tannoy blared out a message that our moves were postponed and we spent the day lazing around. In the evening it started to rain but this did not deter the rats and mice which populated the place in some numbers. They spent the night running around disturbing everyone and ate some of the special biscuits allocated for the sea crossing. Next morning we were brought to 40 minutes stand-by, but in the afternoon it was relaxed to 90 minutes and at a quarter past eleven that night the domestic vehicle echelon was dragged out of bed to be ready to move in 30 minutes. The signals vehicle echelon was not required so we all went off to sleep again.

The domestic echelon travelled off through the night and arrived at the preliminary embarkation area at about four o'clock in the morning, everyone dozed in the vehicles and breakfast was distributed by the Army from lorries at 07.30. Sympathetic residents from the nearby houses came out at intervals with hot tea or cocoa and invited some of the lads in for a wash and shave. The unit medical orderly LAC Macdonald did a good trade on the pavement giving last minute haircuts. An issue of seasickness pills was made and the vehicles moved off to the embarkation point at two o'clock where the final bit of 'snugging' or waterproofing was done. Loading of the landing ship was not complete until 18.15 by which time the convoy had missed the tide.

I was back with the signals vehicles and we were called forward immediately after breakfast and drove to the embarkation area arriving there by 10.30. The news of the invasion of France had had a heartening effect on the civilian population and we were given enthusiastic waves by people as we were obviously on our way to join the invasion forces. I think our odd shaped and overloaded aerial vehicles earned us more interest and applause than the standard vehicles. There was a lot of hanging around and the vehicles were embellished in chalk by some who fancied themselves as artists. One was marked 'Un cage pour Hitler' to explain the wire mesh of the aerial vehicle, a large 'Kemp's Circus' sign was drawn on the Ops vehicle and a smaller equivalent in somebody's French of the current expression 'Hoist up the ladder Jack, I'm fireproof'.

Due to the need to take all the signals personnel with the signals vehicles we had a number of men without transport. They were called twice in error marching to the hards and back again all to no purpose. As a result they missed dinner. The third call was lucky and we followed the enormous numbered and lettered direction signs to the hards. To our surprise when we reached our loading hard it was empty and we had to wait a short time until the landing craft came in.

We had practised dry loading so often that our drivers were confident and capable. All went smoothly and the vehicles were backed one by one in reverse convoy order up the steep ramp on to the craft. It only took ten minutes in all and then the ramp was lifted and the craft backed off and went out to take up position in its shipping convoy. Due to the tide it was 21.00 before the convoy sailed.

The LCT was no more than a long floating straight sided flat bottomed box with a ramp at one end that was raised when at sea. At the other end there was a small bridge, funnel and minimal crew quarters. Our twelve vehicles completely filled the craft. They were all facing the ramp ready to drive off the moment the craft reached the shore and the ramp was lowered. We had each been given a ration pack for the trip including a tin of soup which had a piece of wick sticking out the top. When the wick was lit it glowed and eventually the temperature of the soup was brought up nearly to boiling point. It was a good arrangement but we could have done with a bit of training in its use as I burnt myself on it.

The captain of the craft was a young sub-lieutenant RNVR. I spent some time with him and he explained what was going on. One of the most impressive things about the invasion was the vast number of everything. Our craft anchored off Spithead was one of a line of ten, but when we sailed there were eight lines of ten identical craft in the convoy. The only sleep we were to get was huddled in the vehicles. The weather was fine and clear and the sea calm. After we had turned on to our southerly course it was a very impressive sight to see so many craft on each side in lines. Although it was calm there was a gentle pitching motion and one could see a ripple travel from one end of the craft to the other as the plates gave. I thought I would not want to be on board if the weather got bad at any time.

At some time during the night away out on the horizon there was bit of small arms fire but it did not move any closer. A single aircraft droned overhead, the noise changed and I could hear it diving and then there was silence as though it had dived into the sea. I could not think what had happened to it as there had been no anti-aircraft fire. At 10.30 the next morning we saw the French coast and then slowly made out the vast amount of shipping and naval vessels some of which were firing at unseen targets well inland.

Because of the state of the tide we held off for some time. Eventually we moved slowly forward towards the beach passing some of the big cargo ships and saw the DUKW amphibious vehicles in action for the first time as they moved in and out from the shore unloading the ships. We saw the buildings of the small village backing on to the beach on which we were to land becoming steadily clearer and larger. On the beach we could pick out a few wrecked LCTs and assault craft and assorted debris, an indication of the resistance that the Germans had put up against the initial landings. To our immediate left there were two LCTs close together unloading on to the beach and another on our right. The nearest one to us on our left started to back off, as it did so it commenced to turn and its bows swinging round ripped off all the steel rails of the other craft alongside it.

I ordered everyone into their vehicles and the engines were started. The securing chains on the vehicles were released by the ship's crew; the ramp was partially lowered and as the landing craft grounded on the beach so it was fully lowered. I led the way ashore across the ramp which was fully two feet above the water and we drove on to a sandy beach. The time was 16.00 on the 11th June and we had landed on Love beach near Arsennes sur Mer.

Note: The unit war diary records Arsennes sur Mer but in the humour of the day this was just 'The Back of Beyond.'

As I drove onto the beach I was astonished to see two RAF Police forming part of the Beach Party responsible for guiding assault landing parties of men and vehicles to the beach exits and generally keeping the beaches clear. They directed us across the small length of beach to a narrow exit which had been reinforced with metal tracking. Our big overloaded vehicles carrying the radar aerials were driven slowly and carefully up the steep exit from the beach and through the narrow winding lane to an assembly area in a small paddock at the edge of the village. We felt a bit apprehensive as we had no knowledge of the local ground situation. Were we in any danger of ground attacks? Of shelling? Sniper fire and so on? Would we be allowed to move off to the site pin-point we had been given which was at Periers-sur-le-Ouan five miles north of Caen?

The immediate action was to get the vehicles dispersed around the field, cover them with camouflage netting and remove the waterproofing making them fit to travel some distance again. I went off to find out what the situation was. Within a few minutes I had obtained a number of answers to my questions and was able to pass some of them on to others who had just landed and were equally uninformed. It seemed that there were no known dangers from any enemy activity in the immediate vicinity but a recce of our proposed site was advisable. There was no news of the whereabouts of the other half of the unit so I decided to take the jeep with Bill and Hoppy to recce the site we had been given and was grateful of the offer of a motor cycle escort by the 83 Provost and Security Unit to help us on our way.

Our little party made its way slowly along the narrow country roads delayed by the heavy traffic of assorted Army vehicles that threw up clouds of dust. We saw for the first time the signs of war, small heaps of abandoned clothing, water bottles, ammunition and weapons and the odd rifle stuck muzzle down in the ground with a helmet on the top signifying the recently dug grave. There were a few shelled buildings and each village church spire we saw had a shell hole in it where the Army had sought to get rid of enemy artillery spotting points. We passed a lot of Canadians with their big regimental patches on their arms and they shouted greetings at us when they saw the RAF markings on the vehicles. We turned southwards off the main road on to a small road towards our pin-point and the traffic suddenly thinned. We drove on for about half a mile and found ourselves on a large open space of arable land without hedges that sloped gently down to the south towards enemy held country. There was nothing to be seen, no movement at all and we felt very exposed. We went back a bit and spoke with an Army unit who told us that a tank battle was going on about a mile to the east. We decided that although it was an excellent site we could not set up the convoy without being reasonably certain that it would be shelled and destroyed. We set off back to the landing point and just as we reached the main road we saw a 15cwt. van belonging to the GCC coming from the right. We stopped to exchange news and were greeted with the remark from Flight Lieutenant Gibson of the GCC who was in the vehicle, "Everyone has been looking for you," and were told that we should report to the advanced party of the GCC whose location he gave us.

When we reached the GCC I went in to report to the Group Captain and was totally unprepared for the violent dressing down I was to get. Why had I disobeyed orders and not reported to the GCC on landing? What did I mean by my irresponsible and idiotic behaviour of going to a site that was not yet safely in British hands? I protested in vain that the only orders I had were to set up the equipment at the location that I had been given; that I had not been given the GCC location and had had no orders to report there. My conscience was quite clear on the matter and I wondered why the Group Captain was in such an edgy mood and concluded that he felt very vulnerable without our air picture in front of him. After a bit more harangue he told me that a new site would be found for us and as it was getting late I should return to my unit and move off in the morning.

Back with the signals echelon everyone was anxious to hear about the new site but we were not able to say much other than it was not yet safe enough to be occupied. There had been some discoveries made by airmen rummaging around the field whilst we had been away. They had found a well camouflaged underground bunker made with wooden posts supporting a roof that had been completely covered with earth and grassed over. There were also lots of German ammunition boxes lying around but they all seemed to be filled with exercise ammunition with wooden or fibre bullets. The manner in which the ammunition was packed for easy access was most impressive making our standard wood

59

and tin boxes crude by comparison.

The big discovery was of four beautifully made model tanks about three feet long. We puzzled for a while over their use but on lifting the hatches we found they were packed with explosive. They were in fact the German wire-guided Goliath missiles for the destruction of strong points. I felt more relaxed when Bill disconnected the wires to the explosive charges. As soon as it got dark there was the sound of aircraft and the Army opened up with every type of weapon from all around. It seemed a wise precaution to sleep rough under the vehicles hoping they would protect us from falling shrapnel.

Early next morning I went off to the GCC at Bazenville to find out about our new site. I was delighted to find our other echelon safe and well at the GCC having beached safely on 'Jig' beach the previous day at 17.30. They had landed dry and had been taken to the advanced GCC site for the night. Their crossing on the American LST had been quite luxurious since they had been fed 'in sumptuous style' and had slept well. They made up for that at the GCC where they had had a bad night and were forced to breakfast off their 24-hour emergency rations.

The new site allotted to us called Beaupigny was two or three miles east of Bayeux. It was designated as an Army ammunition dump and was well away from any village. There was a fairly good spot for the Type 11 on the northern edge of the area where the ground sloped gently away to the east and south. Across about 200 yards of growing cereals there was a large flat grass field bordered by trees which would make a good domestic site and also a place for the Type 15 when it arrived. We collected all the unit and set up the radar which was operational by 13.00 that same day (12th June).

The grass paddock made an excellent domestic site and we kept the tents in one corner and dispersed the R/T and W/T vehicles along the edges of the field under the trees and ran the usual telephone lines. We were now all set to carry out the task for which we had trained for so long in the UK. We fully expected that the Luftwaffe would launch massive attacks on the bridgehead and were looking forward to carrying out our first live interceptions of enemy aircraft.

We worked out the watch keeping roster and plotted aircraft tracks steadily to the GCC through the day. We even handled a few defensive patrols of a couple of fighter aircraft with orders to keep them away from the shipping as the navy fired at anything they saw and there had already been casualties as a result. We watched the radar trace rotate four times a minute all day but there was no activity by the Luftwaffe and we were very surprised to be told at 20.30 that we could stand down until 07.00 the next day. Night defence was the responsibility of No. 85 Base Defence Group but we were surprised that GCC did not keep us plotting all night.

As soon as it was really dark there was the noise of an aircraft. It sounded as though it was fairly high and the Army heavy anti-aircraft guns opened up. This was to be expected but it was also a signal for every one in the bridgehead to open up with every weapon they had and there was the ludicrous sight of small arms tracer going up from places all around against an aircraft miles out of range and which could not be seen. It was a noisy night and obviously there was considerably more danger to us from falling shrapnel than from enemy bombs. The waste of ammunition was unbelievable.

Next day we were allocated our aircraft plotting area from 145 degrees round to 310 degrees which was probably our best area as we had a bit of high ground and trees that restricted radar coverage to the north. The adjutant went off to locate the supply bases for food, petrol and oil and I went with Hoppy to have a look at Bayeux and to see what was going on around us. Bayeux turned out to be a quiet little town and we walked down the main street translating the signs for butcher and baker and so on. We had a few words with young children who were asking for chocolate and then cigarettes. I asked one lad why he wanted cigarettes and he said, "Pour Papa" and when I enquired where his father was he told me he was a prisoner of war! We entered a café and called for two glasses of white wine which cost us fifteen francs and we paid for it with new military currency which was looked at with some suspicion. The wine was very sharp and not to our liking, it seemed a bit expensive when we converted the price into English money. There was hardly another serviceman to be seen in the town which seemed not to have suffered any war damage.

We left the town and drove a mile or so to the south-west just to see what was going on and passed a few newly dug graves on the roadside and came across again that nasty sweet smell of the dead with which we were to get accustomed. It looked difficult country to fight in with the narrow lanes and high hedges behind which any enemy could hide. Back at the domestic site the adjutant had returned with good news that he had located all his supply bases and the water bowser had been filled. Not only that but he had arranged for supplies of milk and eggs from the local farm! This was a bit of a surprise as we had all been led to believe that one of the main aims of the invasion was the relief of starving

Europe.

After the heavy anti-aircraft fire of the previous night it seemed a reasonable precaution to 'dig-in'. Most of us had acquired lightweight camp beds in which two assembled jointed metal rods were fitted into the sides of a basic canvas strip which in turn was made rigid by four sprung metal rod supports that kept the whole a few inches off the ground. I marked out in my tent a space big enough to take the bed and dug down a foot or so and placed the bed in it. I then covered the space with wooden pieces taken from old ration boxes and piled the earth I had dug out back on top. I now felt reasonably free from 'friendly' falling shrapnel.

I went round and had a look at each of the sections of the unit and all seemed content and happily settled in. The kitchen was in full working order, the dining marquee was up as were the Sick Quarter tent, MT and latrines. The R/T and W/T sections were comfortable and well camouflaged. LAC Parker one of the radar fitters walked past me at the entrance to the field heading for the main road. I wondered where he was going and stopped him and asked, "Where are you off to Parker?"

"The tech site, Sir," he said. I was baffled as the tech site was only about 200 yards away but was across the field about a hundred and twenty degrees off the direction he was going.

"But the tech site is over there," I said.

"Yes, Sir, I know," he said and looked a bit embarrassed. I was more puzzled than before as Parker was one of our very reliable airmen.

"Well why are you going that way?" I asked, pointing to the way he was heading. He then told me that he was reluctant to go straight across the field because of the warnings we had had at our briefings on mines and boobytraps and he intended therefore, going round by road which was about four times the distance. I assured him that I had walked over the direct path across the fields several times and that I was sure it was safe, whereupon he seemed relieved and promptly walked across to use it. After this incident, I made sure that on our arrival at any new site my jeep was the leading vehicle and I drove into the field before anyone else and got out and walked around. It ensured that there was never any hesitation on the part of others to follow and probably saved some a lot of worry. In most cases I had been there the previous day on my siting expedition, so I was quite sure by then that it was safe.

Over the next few days the weather continued fine with no enemy activity during the day but the usual noisy nights. I found out the location of the 85 Group GCI commanded by Robin McCall and went off to visit him. He was pleased to see me and told me how he had landed successfully on D-Day, his unit being among the first ashore. He had had no casualties although one of his Army sentries had been killed by sniper fire. Robin told me that he was under considerable pressure from senior officers standing at his shoulder all the time and was shortly to be sent back to the UK as the result of a disagreement with them. The other 85 Group GCI which attempted to land on Omaha beach had lost most of its vehicles when trying to go ashore. All the night defence was therefore being done by Robin's unit with night fighters being flown out from the UK. It is a pity that we were not offered the opportunity to help.

There had been a change in the unit status. Base Personnel Staff Office posted the whole of the unit to the strength of the GCC. Not having been informed by GCC, who had been our parent unit, concerning our entitlement to NAAFI packs for overseas, bottles of whisky for officers and SNCOs and rum for the trip across the Channel, we wondered if we would be any better off!

The food we were living on and would continue to live on for some time was the 'Compo Pack' of fourteen man one day rations. These came in eight variations labelled with letters A to H and were in a standard size pack made of hardboard or plywood with softwood batten reinforcement. Each pack contained food to cover all the meals for one day. I have heard some harsh criticism of these rations but they kept us warm and well fed. Most of the contents were packed in tins but the cooks took over the catering and the cooking was done on the pumped petrol stoves that sent out roaring jets of flame under the slatted metal cooking rack on which the dixies were stood.

The meat meals that were available to us varied through stewed beef, steak and kidney pudding, oxtail stew, Lancashire hotpot, vegetable stew, casseroled pork and corned beef. The puddings or sweets were usually variations of suet pudding such as treacle, fig or queen's pudding although there was fruit salad and peaches as well. Items supplied for breakfast or high tea were bacon which came in thin fat slices rolled between sheets of greaseproof paper, cheese, pilchards, tomatoes and skinless sausages all in tins. Of course there was no bread which many of the men missed most of all. Its place was taken by small flat very hard biscuits measuring about two inches by two and a half. To make these palatable there were tins of butter and various jams. There was also a ration of cigarettes, seven per man and boiled sweets or chocolate. Tea came as a powder ground up with dried milk and sugar.

Criticisms and preferences were soon established. There was some difficulty in getting used to the tea. Our water collected in the 250 gallon water bowser came from heavily chlorinated Army supply points. When the tea/sugar/ milk powder was added the resultant product had a curdled appearance and a taste that was quite unique but later was always welcome at any hour day or night. I found the rations most satisfactory although the casseroled pork was very fat and a bit too rich for me, the thin fat bacon was not very attractive and the cheese whilst tasty burned the skin off my mouth. The lack of bread was a bit of a shock and was to result in our first casualty of the campaign when one of the radar fitters broke his dentures on the hard biscuits and was to be toothless for weeks.

Travelling on the Normandy roads meant being covered in the fine dust sent up by the Army trucks that jammed them. One's shirt was filthy within an hour and it did not take long for most of us to seek out a French civilian near by who was willing to do our laundry. There were those of us who used our half-forgotten schooldays French but those who waved a bar of soap and held their dirty laundry in their hands made themselves understood just as well and got the same service.

As more squadrons of fighters became available in the bridgehead we were given the task of air surveillance of squadrons carrying out offensive sweeps hoping to stir up reaction from the German air force. On the 19th June the weather broke giving low cloud and rain, but a single enemy raider took a chance and flew over the Caen area in the cloud the following day. When the weather improved on the 22nd activity by the *Luftwaffe* started to increase. We plotted 20 plus enemy aircraft for 280 miles as they flew at 10,000 feet from Le Havre to the Cherbourg Peninsula and then south-east. There was no reaction to the raid by GCC. In the afternoon we controlled 441 and 442 Squadrons on a sweep and they claimed six enemy aircraft destroyed without loss. In the evening a Fortress flew over on fire and we watched six crew leave the aircraft by parachute before the wing folded and the aircraft fell out of the sky. One man came down uninjured not far away.

The next few days were fairly quiet involving only routine plotting apart from a single German aircraft that crashed in flames just over a mile away. It had not been plotted so we assume it had been on a low level mission. We were doing most of our controlling with Canadian Spitfire squadrons vectoring them into a bunch of 30 hostiles on the 28th. The best day was the last day of the month when we twice intercepted enemy formations over the Falaise area and six enemy aircraft were claimed as destroyed.

The tension in the operations room could change in an instant. The radar operators reporting the air picture continuously watched the aerial trace as it rotated four times each minute. They watched for hours an empty area of enemy sky or tracked the friendly aircraft flying over it on their offensive missions. However, when a new echo appeared on the radar and the magic words 'New track' were spoken, the tension in the ops room rose. The heightfinder operator would swing his aerial round on to the raid and the excitement would continue until the new track was recognized as friendly or the hostile had been intercepted. For the controller the operation of a defensive patrol of fighters up and down a pre-ordered line on the map was a quiet routine with a regular R/T transmission to the formation leader of 'Nothing to report'. However, on the appearance of a new track there was an immediate change of situation. The fighters were given immediate warning of the direction and range of the incoming threat and ordered to turn on to a new heading to intercept. The controller then with half an eye overlooking his heightfinder's display, which would hopefully give the height of the incoming raid, an indication of its strength, if the enemy were flying at different levels and a relative height between our fighters and the enemy formation continued with his interception orders and information to the pilots.

Although there had been no liaison between the fighter pilots and ourselves and they had little or no idea of the capabilities of our radar, we gave the small formations a confident and continuous flood of information on the enemy raid during the short time of the interception, the enemy height, range, direction, numbers, and as they got closer the bearing and range from our fighters and relative height.

There were many patrols that were uneventful but when hostile aircraft were picked up on the radar one could feel the excitement within the ops cabin and indeed in the R/T vehicles where the operators always listened in. We were all very happy doing our best to put the fighter pilots in contact with the enemy, giving them hopefully the benefit of preparation and surprise. We were at last seeing successes in the job for which we had trained for so long.

We were now into July on our first site in Normandy and we could look back with a certain amount of satisfaction on all that had happened to the unit in June. We had made our transition from a unit under training to a successful operational unit. We had successfully crossed the Channel and landed in the Normandy beach-head without casualties, in fact not a single vehicle had even got its tires wet.

Conditions had not been all that we hoped or feared. There had been no obvious danger from enemy ground action, dangers from night bombing seemed to be less than that from the Army's falling shrapnel and spent small arms ammunition coming from the sky. We were feeding well with four hot meals a day but so far there was no bread, not many cigarettes and no beer. The small echelon with our Type 15 radar had not yet arrived in Normandy so the unit was not yet complete.

The main operations room duties that of reporting the air picture and the provision of height and other information to help the controllers in their interception work, was the responsibility of the Radar Operators and they had performed their job well. Perhaps we were a little disappointed not to be able to 'have a go' at night raiders but after all we were part of 83 Group whose task was a daytime one. The opening days had been quiet but the enemy activity towards the end of June provided everyone with excitement and the thrill of success when enemy aircraft were intercepted and much of the pilots' R/T chatter could be heard by the radar and R/T operators. As might be expected, a score sheet or chart was painted inside the ops room on which the successes of the unit measured by enemy aircraft destroyed by fighters under our control were listed.

The admin and back-up sections of the unit were doing a fine job and like any other small unit where morale is good the sections shared their experiences and discussed them during meals and in their sleeping tents. The fighter pilots' successes against the *Luftwaffe* were shared by all, cooks and MT drivers knew all about them and spoke of them as their own. Our operational working hours had changed and plotting generally ceased just before midnight and started again at 04.30. Early in July we had our telephone lines cut for the first time by one of the trucks that was bringing ammunition into the ever growing arms dump in the middle of which our radar was sited. That meant that we had to switch over to plotting by W/T which was not very satisfactory, and of course we lost the plain language line needed to arrange the takeover of aircraft and other liaison necessary with the GCC. Fortunately the Air Formation Signals were quickly on the job of repair of the line.

The work of controlling for much of the day now consisted of operating a standing patrol of a section of fighters on 'Beach Patrol'. They were in fact kept away from the beach to prevent the Navy from using them as target practice! Whilst there was little enemy activity, that is we only had a successful interception and combat about every other day, there were lots of reports of enemy aircraft which often turned out to be our own fighters. All Army units who had guns capable of firing against aircraft did so at almost every opportunity whether the aircraft were hostile or not. As an example, on July 7th six Typhoons passed over our site and they were being fired at as they came out of the American sector and the firing was taken up by the British guns and later I heard by the light ack-ack on their own airfield.

On that same day we saw two waves of Lancaster and Halifax aircraft escorted by twelve Spitfire squadrons attacking targets in the Caen area. A Mosquito aircraft crashed not far away the pilot having been seen to bale out but there was no news of the navigator. Aircraft crashes near our site became quite common as a Typhoon came down near by some two days later and the pilot stepped out unhurt.

It was also a busy day administratively as Group ordered us to take a Summary of Evidence on the breach of security by the Cipher Sergeant back in England before D-Day. Flt. Lt. Hopper did the Summary and after a further long period of waiting the case was eventually passed back to me for disposal. My powers of punishment for an SNCO were limited to a 'Severe Reprimand' which I gave to him and told him that in my opinion he had got off extraordinarily lightly.

Just as we celebrated the end of our fourth week in Normandy so we received the news that live ENSA shows and cinema shows would be available any day. We were already participating in a football league and getting used to the static life. I took a short trip into Bayeux and found it quite changed in character and full of troops. The little children who had asked Hoppy and me for sweets, chocolate and cigarettes were still there but were much better organized. They now dragged sacks behind them to carry the day's takings. For our part we were living well although we decided it was a bit over the top when four out of our five officers arrived at table each with a half litre of cream that we had organized. There was shortly to be an official request from Army Headquarters for all troops to purchase dairy products from the local farmers as they were unable to dispose of them through their normal markets due to communications with the rest of France being cut because of the fighting.

The 14th July was the French National Holiday and Bayeux was *en fête*. I did not go there but the farmer in whose field we had our domestic site entertained some of the lads. It was a special day for the unit and many others as we received the first white bread since the landings which was issued as part of the rations. This was to be followed by our first NAAFI supplies and the first beer for the unit since we left the UK.

Our rear echelon too arrived that same day with the Type 15 having had an uneventful trip. We lined up those vehicles in the paddock ready for assembly and I went along to give a hand. I found I needed another spanner to help with the assembly of the aerial and walked over to the Crossley transmitter vehicle and reached up to the cab handle intending to take a spanner from the toolkit that was normally kept in the cab. To my surprise I got a heavy electric shock and threw myself backwards to free myself from the door handle. I picked myself up, put on my hat again and walked over to the aerial vehicle intending to use its toolkit instead. On grabbing the door handle I got another shock! It was one of the hazards of mobile signals units that the earthing was not always effective.

There were no major air attacks by the *Luftwaffe* and the small raids that did approach were intercepted by the small continuous defensive patrols that were maintained. We had now to share these with 15053 and 8024 the other two FDPs. The bridge-head was now overcrowded with every type of unit many of which were not fighting units but cinemas and so on for entertainment of the troops. There was a general feeling of disappointment that so little forward progress was being made by the Army. When the troops were held up they asked for support from the heavy bombers and then complained that the bombing had destroyed the roads so that they could not get through with their tanks and vehicles! We had been static too long and were itching to move forward.

The Army had reported that they had been attacked by German low-flying aircraft in the Tilly-sur-Seulles area and I was asked by GCC if I would go out there and act as a Forward Control Point. That meant taking a ground to air R/T vehicle and calling the fighters in by visual directions when the low flying aircraft appeared. I went to a gently sloping site that gave a clear view of the land to the south and sat down in a comfortable chair in the sunshine and waited hoping to see some action. The R/T vehicle was close by and I had a microphone to speak to the fighters should I need to. In front of us was a battery of 25-pounder guns and I was interested in the way they operated. The gunners were called together and received a briefing rather like an American football team. They then walked back to their guns and fired them off either all together or in a running salvo or at intervals. There seemed to be nothing coming back from the Germans. The weather was fine and sunny but nothing happened and I felt bored.

I wandered off a short way and found a magnificent German bunker dug into the field, roofed with turf and fitted with timber bedding clear of the floor. It was empty and clean, not apparently ever having been occupied. I also had a look at a large field to the back of us and found that it had been shelled with instantaneous exploding shells as one could just see the marks in the grass. The marks overlapped and thousands of shells must have been expended, but I saw no signs of German dug-outs, or litter, or occupation. I noticed an Army unit some way off and went over to find some tanks and crews in what they termed their 'harbour'. The tank crews explained that they were operating at night and came back to their harbour to sleep and eat and do maintenance.

It was getting dark and there was still no activity so I announced that I proposed to go and sleep in the German bunker. The R/T crew was horrified and spoke of booby traps and lice. I went therefore to sleep alone in the huge bunker and had a good night's rest. When I got up in the morning I asked the others what sort of a night they had had. They told me they had had a dreadful night with no sleep at all, as the guns from both sides had been going off all the time. I did some more sunbathing waiting for German low flying attackers which never came and was then recalled and returned to 15054.

The GCC was only a few miles from us so I was able to visit them at fairly regular intervals. I was invited over when Winston Churchill visited them on his tour round the bridge-head and listened to him as he said a few encouraging words. I was very surprised to see how tired and worn out he looked. Thinking back at the time I decided he had had responsibility enough to kill most men. It was at the GCC one day that I was talking to the Medical Officer when an airman passed and the MO said, "If that man comes to me again I'll charge him with malingering." I was astonished by the MO's remark as I recognized the airman as one of my own men who had fairly recently arrived from the UK having been part of the rear echelon. The story was that in the road at Emsworth where the convoy had been left was a house in which two ex-ATS girls were living having been discharged by the Army for some offence or other. The airman had got friendly with one of the girls and had apparently had his first sexual relations with her. Having been lectured at Renscombe on the dangers of such activities he bathed himself with disinfectant using it a bit stronger than recommended just to ensure that it would be efficacious. The next day he inspected his penis to see if all was well and thinking that it looked a bit pinker than usual he proceeded to bathe it with even stronger disinfectant. The result was his frequent trips to the MO. I think the MO's words must have had an effect as I heard no more of the matter or maybe our own medical orderly gave the airman some words of wisdom.

Life on the technical site was getting very uncomfortable as the arms dump was increasing in size daily as more and more trucks arrived with ammunition for stockpiling. Not only were the trucks cutting our telephone lines quite regularly but when I went up one day at watch change I found that a number of heavy trucks had parked so close to the aerial that there was barely room for it to turn which would have almost entirely destroyed its ability to detect aircraft. I got the trucks moved immediately but the site for us was now almost unusable. There was in addition the added fear that we were living in the middle of this great ammunition dump which might blow up any time due to enemy action or some accidental reason.

The operations staff officer at Group Headquarters who was responsible for recommending or approving siting arrangements was a Canadian squadron leader called Macgregor or 'Mac' for short. When at last the Army was reported as making some gains in the Villers Bocage area, Mac decided it was time we could look for a more forward site especially as ours at Beaupigny was rapidly becoming untenable. It was to be the sort of risky siting trip for which Mac was to become well known and involve other small units besides ourselves. Mac duly arrived in his jeep to pick up Bill the Canadian technical officer and myself. Mac was dressed in a rather fine twill khaki uniform and I was in my normal coarse khaki British battledress. Bill was in his blue RAF battledress not having been able to get a khaki one in a size big enough to fit him from the limited supplies available to us.

We drove off together in the general direction where we hoped to find a site but found nowhere suitable and finally got lost in the narrow winding lanes. We passed a single soldier who was using a mine detector

70

to sweep the grass verges and asked him which way the front line was. He looked a bit vague and then pointed in the direction from which we had come! We decided to drive on a bit further and came across a farm on our right where I suggested we stopped so that I could enquire our whereabouts. The front door of the farmhouse was only a few yards off the road separated by a small gate and short path. I opened the gate to go in only to retreat rather quickly. Lying on the path was the bloated body of a dead man dressed in civilian clothes.

We drove on a bit further and the narrow lane turned right into an open patch of meadowland and we could see that the small bridge ahead of us had been blown up. Looking over to our right about a hundred yards away were a couple of farm cottages outside of which half a dozen or so soldiers were dancing about in single file following their leader who was wearing a black top hat. We went over to talk to them and they looked a bit foolish as we enquired what they were doing and where the fighting was. The corporal went and got a map and showed us where we were. He then pointed at the steep wooded slope on the other side of the small stream and said, "There's a village up there, our Captain has been up there a couple of times and says the village is being shelled every so often." The corporal did not know which side was shelling the village or anything about what was going on but he agreed to get his men to manhandle our jeep across the little stream.

Over the stream the narrow lane went straight up the steep hill the branches of the trees on each side meeting overhead. I was startled when as we drove slowly up the steep hill I saw a Bren-gun carrier off the road almost hidden in the undergrowth and the soldiers in it dressed in full camouflage. They made no move to stop us and we continued up the hill. I was getting a bit nervous and as we came to the first houses of the village I yelled to Mac, "Turn right at the tee junction," which he did to my relief. The village had appeared deserted but I felt very much happier when we left it without incident. We had just cleared the last houses in the village street when we saw coming slowly towards us in the middle of the road and looking very warlike a single armoured car. It seemed a good time to stop. As we did so a young lieutenant stood up in his scout car and leant over and said, "You chaps are a bit off track, aren't you?" We must have looked a bit odd in our mixed uniforms and our siting story a bit weak. He was rather insistent that we went back with him to his squadron headquarters which he said was not far away. I could tell from the lieutenant's attitude that he was decidedly suspicious about us. The squadron of scout cars was from the 11th Huzzars and was harboured in an orchard not far from the village. We again told our story to the major there and were directed down the road where, it was said, we would be safer.

After a mile or so we came across the Army in some numbers and spoke to a major and his captain about the local situation and a likely place for a site. Mac wanted to take the road right but this went through a wood and did not seem very promising to me. The major agreed that the road would probably be safe but he had not been down it himself. He refused to commit himself about snipers and on my enquiry about possible mines said, "Well, you will see them if they are there." It did not sound very reassuring to me and I was somewhat puzzled when the two officers seemed to lose interest in our conversation and dropped into a ditch alongside the road. Naturally I enquired what was going on. There was a whirring sound overhead and both officers ducked and the major said, "That is one of theirs." I realized then that the whirrings and thumps that I had been hearing meant that shells were dropping somewhere near by.

I had had enough for one day and told Mac to call it a day. We left rather hurriedly raising a cloud of dust which we hope did not bring any more shellfire down on the unit we had left. From this experience I learned that I would have to try and control Mac somewhat if we were not to land up in Germany long before the Army.

It was the first week of August when we moved out of our site at Beaupigny and felt that at last we were making some forward progress. Our new site was at Foulanges some fifteen miles away by direct measurement. We were somewhat disappointed that it was in a south-westerly direction and not as we had hoped towards the east which was our hoped for advance line. The area around Caumont had been static for a long time but the Army were now attacking in force and making some if slow progress. It was a chance to get mobile again and everyone was happy.

72

On the left a Type 15 search radar with IFF interrogator. On the right a Type 13 nodding height finder. Both aerials in final stages of erection and are on the 6 wheeled Austin chassis.

Bruce Robertson collection

A Type 11 search radar aerial. This was later mounted on a six wheeled prime mover.

A Type 15 radar Operations/receiver vehicle on its Crossley chassis.
In the background is a Type 11 aerial on its 6 wheeled Austin chassis.

A Type 13 height finder aerial packed 'ready for the road'

A 'flash' photo of the PPI teller. Note the gridded map.
The operators worked in almost total darkness.

The Type 15 Receiver/Operations Vehicle (Type 409) Exterior

a. The side opening for extension.
b. The rear framework on which the canvas porch was fitted.

c. The air-cooling ducts.
d. The support mast for the feeders together with the five gallon drum to provide tensioning.

Interior

a. The height range display.
b. The PPI on which the controller worked.
c. The aerial turning controls.
d. The navigation table.
e. The telephone PBX.
f. Mounting rails enabling the console to be moved for servicing.

Extract from 'Normandy to the Baltic'
by Field Marshal the Viscount Montgomery of Alamein

Page 147
The German troops were told that the Nijmegen road bridge was the 'gateway to the Fatherland' and that its destruction was essential to avoid defeat. All available land and air forces were committed to the task . . . .

In addition the enemy made a number of determined air attacks to put the Nijmegen bridges out of action, notably on the 27th September when nearly six hundred aircraft appeared over the area. These attacks fortunately failed . . . .

On the night 28/29 September, specially trained swimmers equipped with demolition charges seriously damaged the railway bridge and also caused the road bridge to be closed for twenty-four hours.

Quote from Montgomery's 'Normandy to the Baltic'

Combat Report of Flt. Lt. R.M. Davenport DFC, 5 Oct 44, Holland, on B84, 262 Destruction, 401 Squadron RCAF.

I was flying Yellow 1, 401 Blackout Squadron, when we sighted ME262 at 12,000ft 5m NE of Nijmegen. I waited till he made his final break then came in 20' line astern at approx 450 m.p.h. I gave him a 3 second burst at 400 yards and observed strikes on the fuselage. I then continued the chase which was composed of rolls, dives and turns at approx 275 mph. I finally closed to 300 yds line astern and emptied the remainder of my guns approx 10 or 12 secs into the kite, observing strikes in the engine and fuselage. The a/c was burning all this time. The pilot seemed to be unhurt and put up a good fight during all this, at last realising the fight was up he attempted to ram Red 1, on the way to the ground when he crashed and burned. I claim one 5th ME 262 destroyed.

Note: One Me 262 of 3rd Staffel KG 51, works No. 170093, pilot Hauptmann Hans Christof Buttmann, crashed. The pilot was killed and buried at Holenhoek Military Cemetery.

Combat report of destruction of the ME 262.

ENEMY AIRCRAFT.

Squadron.	Pilot.	Destroyed.	Prob.Dest.	Damaged.
19	F/L. Paton			1 FW.190
122	F/O. Cush	1 Me.109		
174	F/S. McKenzie			1 FW.190
412	F/L. Fox	2 FW.190		1 FW.190
"	"			1 Me.109
"	F/L. Smith	2 Me.109		
"	F/L. Laubman	5 Me.109		1 Me.109
"	"	1 FW.190		1 FW.190
"	F/C. Perryman	3 Me.109		1 FW.190
"	F/O. Jamieson	2 FW.190		
"	F/L. Doak	1 FW.190		
411	F/L. Korts	1 FW.190		1 FW.190
"	F/L. Lapp	2 FW.190		
"	F/O. Mercer	1 FW.190		1 FW.190
"	F/L. McConnell	1 FW.190		
"	F/O. Ireland	1 FW.190		
"	F/O. Fow	1 FW.190		
"	F/O. Reid			1 FW.190
"	F/L. Lapp & F/C. Cook.	1 Me.410		
416	F/L. Harding	1 FW.190		1 Me.109
"	"	1 Me.109		
"	F/L. Sager	1 FW.190		
"	"	1 Me.109		
"	F/L. Cuthbertson	1 FW.190		
"	F/L. Rainville	1 FW.190		
"	F/O. St. George			1 Me.109
"	F/O. Cameron			2 Me.109
"	F/L. Mason			1 FW.190
421	F/L. Mitchener	1 Me.109		
"	F/O. Calvert	1 Me.109		
"	F/O. MacDonald	1 Me.109		
"	F/O. Decourcy			1 Me.109
438	F/O. Upham	1 Me.109		
441	F/L. Blake	1 Me.109		
"	F/L. Copeland	1 Me.109		
"	F/O. Bradman	1 Me.109		
443	W/C. Johnson	1 Me.109		
"	F/O. Gilbert	1 Me.109		
"	F/L. Stovell	1 Me.109	1 Me.109	
"	F/O. Hodgins		1 Me.109	
"	F/L. Fuller	1 Me.109		
"	F/L. Walz	1 Me.109		
453	W/O. Lyall	1 Me.109		
"	F/L. Bennett	1 Me.109		2 Me.109
"	F/O. Marsh	1 Me.109		
"	F/O. Leith	1 Me.109		
"	W/O. Taylor	1 Me.109		2 Me.109
	Totals ...	46	2	20

Page from an 83 Group Daily Intelligence Summary showing fighter claims against enemy aircraft for 27th September 1944.

Self   VE Day Travemünde

'Bill' Jones who kept everything working.

Travemünde All of us.

The 'Hard' Travemünde. Looking east towards the Russian Zone.

The Baltic coast just off the base at Travemünde.

Travemünde. Blohm and Voss 138 flying boats. The Russian Zone in the background.

Travemünde. 'Any more for the Skylark?'

Travemünde. The giant BV 222 with a FW 190.

Travemünde. One of our mini submarines.

Corporal Bluett's watch of radar operators outside the type 11 Ops vehicle. Note the cables.

A V1 store near Leck. The Luftwaffe were allowed to keep an armed guard on the site long after our arrival.

The first Fokke Wolf 190 off the '054 assembly line. Corporal Hancock in the pilot's seat.

Belsen. Survivors

Belsen. Non-survivors

The site at Foulange was pleasantly rural and set above the surrounding countryside. All the fields around had growing crops and the weather was glorious. We had hardly settled in when we were honoured by a visit from our Group Captain at the GCC. He flew in to the site in a light Army spotter aircraft which was a surprise and delight to all of us, as we seldom had occasion to see any aircraft from close up although we talked to the fighter pilots on the radio most of every day. The Group Captain seemed very pleased with what he saw of 15054 and was gracious enough to say so. Hoppy returned from a stint 'up forward' as a Forward Control Point but he like me had seen no enemy air activity to make the trip worth while.

The big news was of the breakout by the Americans from the Cherbourg Peninsula and the great counter-attacks by the Germans in their attempts to drive to the sea and cut the American forces in two. The British Army too seemed to be making progress although it was up to now painfully slow. We had a very disturbed night and day when tanks went past the site in a seemingly unending line throwing up great clouds of dust and creating a great deal of noise. They were off to reinforce the big Army thrust to the south. Our site was apparently right on a cross-country tank track and the whole disturbance was to be repeated two nights later as the deployment of the tanks was reversed.

Operationally we were now less likely to be used for controlling defensive fighter aircraft as we were further south from the bridge-head and a little further west away from the general direction of any incoming *Luftwaffe* attacks. All the fighter bombers were engaged in attacks on tanks and motor transport being used by the Germans in their advance towards Mortain and we were not called upon to give them surveillance or navigational assistance. The local farmer made contact with us and asked for our help with the harvest and the lads were soon pleased to be working in the fields in the warm sunny weather.

We had been on the site just ten days when Mac (83 Group Ops) got in touch and said that in view of the advance by the Army we should be looking for another site. He turned up early the next day and we set off in a south-easterly direction. It was agreed that we would find a suitable site as far forward as we could get on the assumption that by the time we moved the next day the Army would have advanced a little further and it would be 'safe' to operate the radar there.

We soon saw signs of the heavy fighting that had taken place. There were dead horses and cattle here and there on the road and as we passed through a small village we saw where a Bren-gun carrier and a tank had been blown up. The Bren-gun carrier had been destroyed by a mine that had blown a hole through the floor. There was an awful smell of death everywhere. The dead horses and cattle that were caught up in the fighting always seemed to lie with their legs straight up in the air. In the hot weather their bodies turned black and swelled until they were unnaturally round and inflated like a balloon and then they would burst emitting a foul sweet smell that was to linger as the carcass slowly collapsed and went liquid and was finally removed by the work of maggots and rats and birds.

We came across a small wood that ran along a ridge and saw that as our Sherman tanks had pushed their noses out into the clear grassland beyond so each one had been put out of action by enemy anti-tank weapons. I think we counted eight in all. As we drove further south so the signs of the fighting became more recent. There were bodies of dead German soldiers lying beside the road and piles of abandoned hand-grenades, panzerfaust, ammunition and even half-eaten rations and clothing. At one open crossroads a German NCO and three young soldiers had been left in two small slit trenches to hold up the British advance with the aid of their anti-tank rocket. All had been killed.

We drove as far forward as we dared and found a suitable site for the radar near a village called La Villette which was just north of Condé-sur-Noire and some twenty odd miles south-east of our site at Foulanges. Driving back it was agreed that we would move as soon as we had confirmation from the GCC. It had been a pleasant short stop at Foulanges but we were pleased to be on our way again the next day (August 18th). It was an easier move than our previous one as we had not had time to get really static as we had on our first site in Normandy. I was driving through the scenes of fighting for the third time in our way to La Villette but it came as a shock to the rest of the unit who were seeing them for the first time.

The site would have been ideal both technically and domestically if it had not been surrounded by the remains of recent heavy fighting.

There were still unburied bodies of dead German soldiers near by and piles of abandoned weapons and other debris. I saw a fine farm cart with its dead horses lying in their harness. I went to admire it and saw to my astonishment that it was marked with German regimental numbers and wondered if the Germans had had it made as some form of unit recreation. I did not know at the time that the German army had nearly two million horses on active service and relied to a large extent on horse drawn transport for supplies. We had always thought of the German army in terms of blitzkrieg and Tiger tanks and superior weapons not realizing that their army did a lot of marching, used horses and carts for supplies and might well have been envious of our unit where the number of vehicles was almost half the personnel establishment.

I looked in at the local farm which was deserted. There was an awful smell and as I looked into a cattle stall I recoiled as the animals were all dead and their bodies covered with maggots. Whilst some had probably been killed as the result of shelling the remainder chained in the stalls must have died from thirst or starvation. The weather was hot and sunny but eating our meals was hardly enjoyable with a large number of large meat flies and wasps constantly landing on the food. As a counter to the effect of the sight of so many dead animals and Germans the lads had rescued a number of hens and a young goat kid which they wanted to keep especially when the hens in gratitude laid some eggs on the beds in the tents.

In addition to the FDP radars there were Light Warning radar units that had a small short range radar with no height finding capability. They were intended to be used to cover any blind spots in the major radar stations' coverage and were generally attached to the FDP concerned. At this time we were responsible for 6091 LWS and the Flight Sergeant in charge, F/S Mitchell and a co-driver drove off to find a new site. We then received a report that the vehicle had run over a mine and whilst the vehicle was a write off no one was hurt. I went out and saw what had happened. The vehicle had been travelling down a narrow road in a gulley when it ran over the mine. The force of the explosion blew the rear wheel off and upwards so that it lodged in the branches of a tree on the steep embankment. Those in the vehicle were very lucky not to have been killed.

We were offered by the GCC, two places at a rest camp which had been opened at Port-en-Bessin. Whilst none of us could be said to be suffering from battle fatigue we were unlikely to get many perks passed on to us from the GCC so we accepted with thanks and Cpl. Lithgow a radar fitter and one of the older members of the unit and LAC Banham a popular radar operator who had a bit of a weight problem went off for their rest. We wondered at the time how they would find their way back to us.

The Army had by now really broken out of the bridge-head and had started the mad rush across France. We had only been a few days at La Villette when we were on the move again. Before we left the site I noticed that the live chicken had all been pushed into the long wire mesh box that formed the IFF interrogator of the Type 15 radar and the young goat was tethered and travelling in the back of one of the three-tonners. I thought that perhaps the unit was living up a bit too realistically to its title 'Kemp's Circus' but it was good for morale after the nasties that we had seen at La Villette. This time we advanced forty miles still in a south-easterly direction to a site above the village of Fontenai on the edge of the Foret D'Ecouves half-way between Argentan and Alencon. By some mischance of timing we had been ordered back into our blue uniforms and on seeing us a young lad ran through the village yelling, "*Les Boches sont revenus.*" It was not a good start.

We were now well south of the British Zone and we cheered men of General Leclerc's French Army as they drove past us in their armoured carriers. I went down to the village and enquired after the mayor and was directed to the house of the mayoress. I asked what celebrations the village was arranging after the announcement (premature) of the relief of Paris. Apparently they had none planned but we persuaded the people to turn up that evening in the village hall for some sort of celebration. We then helped round up some horses that were running loose on the road and when I was told that they were German Army horses I decided to make a present of them to a farmer who told me that he had had his own horses commandeered. He seemed most grateful to me.

A good number of the unit turned up at the village hall that night but things were a bit starchy at first partly due to language troubles and partly to the natural suspicion of people to any invader under the guise of liberator or not. However, a large number of bottles of wine and Calvados were broached and officers, airmen and natives all seemed to enjoy themselves. I remember someone producing a bottle of Calvados of odd shape covered with cobwebs and assuring me that it was more than a hundred years old. We were also presented with several other bottles of wine or the famous Calvados. As the CO I had been obliged to exchange rather more toasts than some of the others and I found it necessary to hand over to Hoppy the job of driving my three-tonner back

76

to the site. Not everyone was for the British as we found out. Two fine new waterproof mackintoshes that we had used to black out the hall disappeared and were never found.

The next day a unit of the RAF Regiment arrived to give us a bit of protection as German troops were reported still active and in hiding in the forest. A small 'Y' unit also arrived in preparation for a new role for us, that of acting as a temporary or forward GCC until the main unit could move. This would mean having some of the planning staff officers with us and telephone lines from forward airfields being laid to the unit so that we could pass the operational tasking orders to them and give what surveillance and service we could. The 'Y' unit listened in on the German fighter aircraft R/T frequencies which meant that we would know when the *Luftwaffe* fighters were airborne. In addition, since the 'Y' could also by direction finding give a bearing on the enemy transmissions, the aircraft plot could be recognized on the radar.

The pressure was now on the domestic support side of the unit to keep us supplied with food, diesel oil, petrol and drinking water. With such a rush forward the old Army supply depots were out of reach and the location of the new ones unknown or else if located they were unwilling or unable to supply us. Bill Jones and the adjutant went off that day back to the GCC to finalize arrangements for our move and operation as forward GCC and also to obtain what supplies could be had. The bad news was that the NAAFI had no beer.

Our stay at Fontenai was the shortest ever, just three days before we were off again to a new site at Grossoevres by St Andrê in the German airfield complex at Evreux. When we arrived we had no contact with anyone. The expected planners, Army liaison officers and extra signals units had not arrived. We set up the radar and opened up nevertheless on the R/T channels passing information on some enemy formation picked up by the 'Y' unit and its position located on the radar. We were very gratified when someone acknowledged our R/T transmission and seemed pleased to have the information.

The GCC planners, signals units and two units of RAF Regiment armoured cars arrived and our cooks served over 1,000 meals that day, about four times our usual number. The Air Formation Signals unit ran in telephone lines from the advanced airfields and we were launched into our new role as the forward GCC. Our operations vehicles had to be adapted to show the states of squadron aircraft and the missions on which their aircraft were detailed. We lined up an empty three-ton GP close alongside the Type 11 Ops vehicle and backed both of them on to the opening in the side of the Type 15 Ops vehicle. There was now one large operational space in which we could have a General Situation raid map as well as the new tote boards.

In addition to Hoppy, Monty and myself many of the ops NCOs were co-opted into the job of deputy controllers to provide listening watches and to relay information on the R/T channels. Additional logs had to be kept of the orders that were being passed to the squadrons and of current events. It would be an understatement to say we were busy, we were stretched to the limit.

The adjutant again went off early in the morning in search of food for us. Because of the rapid advance of the Army, forward food depots were hard to find and when they were found the officers in charge of them were once again reluctant to issue much in the way of rations to small RAF units. After much argument between a Lt. Col. CRASC and a Major of 16 BSD Flying Officer Taylor returned victorious with rations for four days.

After just two days the GCC contingent and the RAF Regiment units with their armoured cars all disappeared suddenly with hardly a word of farewell. Word came in of the continued advance by the Army and the crossing of the Seine which meant that our present site would soon be too far in the rear. Our next move was to be aimed at the area around Beauvais where the *Luftwaffe* had another group of airfields. Those of the unit who had made contact with locals in their search for eggs reported that they had been made to feel very unwelcome. The *Luftwaffe* had apparently built up a good relationship in the area and had also married many of the local girls. Our driving out of the Germans was not appreciated there at that time.

The chicken which had been transported from the last site had fallen into disfavour with some of the men in the unit. Whilst there were those who were happy to have eggs laid on their beds, there were others who objected strongly when the chicken left rather less welcome marks. It was agreed that the chicken would be better appreciated by all if they went in the pot and they were handed over to the cooks for preparation. The young goat too had developed objectionable habits one of which was running up the fly sheets of the tents and standing on the ridge poles. The tents had served us well and I thought it was wrong to run the risk of having them damaged so I asked who had adopted the kid to find a good home for it.

On the last day of August I went off very early with Bill to look for our next site near to Beauvais. We drove about twenty miles to Vernon where we joined the queue of vehicles waiting to cross the river Seine over the temporary pontoon bridge that the Army had built across it. This was the first big river that we were to cross and it was strange driving across the temporary pontoon bridge only a foot or so above the water. There were again signs of recent heavy fighting and as we slowly climbed up the steep winding road from the bridge through the woods that overlooked the river we could see the bodies of several German soldiers lying on the ground or in open trenches between the trees. We drove on for about forty miles beyond the bridge and after looking around for a while found a good site at a place called La Vauroux. It was getting dark as we returned to the unit after a very long and tiring day.

We still had the small 'Y' unit with us and also a point-to-point radio link unit which was most helpful as it meant that we could get into immediate speech contact with the GCC without waiting for landlines to be laid. In addition it was better than our W/T link as it had a longer working range.

Having packed up yet again we set off with the whole convoy for the new site. The temporary pontoon bridge over the Seine seemed very unstable as it sagged under the weight of each of the vehicles as it moved across and I am sure every driver like myself felt a little anxious at the movement with the vehicle only just above the water. Our vehicles especially the aerials were generally overloaded and had to be driven most carefully especially over the slightest bit of uneven road, narrow lanes or sharp bends. As we climbed slowly up the steep road from the bridge I passed for the third time a camouflaged uniform in the road which all the vehicles ahead of me carefully drove around. It was only then that I realized that the uniform was in fact a dead German soldier who must have lain there for some days and it was the third time that I was passing the spot. In the woods there were now teams of civilians digging graves for the dead under the supervision of the Army.

At La Vauroux we set up the equipment and the domestic site and commenced working normally. The locals made contact with us and those calling themselves the Maquis went off with a few of the lads who came back with a captured German prisoner. This effort was completely upstaged by LAC Coogan one of our drivers who went out on a duty run and came back with his three-tonner loaded up with forty-eight prisoners. We handed the prisoners over to the Army and decided that having taken a number of prisoners we had proved our point, we were in the forefront of the advance. The taking of prisoners was however a distraction from our main task and we made a decision to ignore any nonbelligerent German military personnel from then on, leaving them to be picked up by those units that were following up.

A young RAF Sergeant Air Gunner was brought to me. He explained that he was the sole survivor from a Halifax that had been shot down and that since then he had been living with a young Frenchwoman who had sheltered him in one of the nearby villages. He said that there had been German troops billeted in the same village and he was sure that they knew of his presence there but did nothing about it. The Air Gunner was still suffering from shock and was very worried about being sent back on operational flying. We handed him over to the Army to arrange for his repatriation. The sufferings of the civilians in the south of England were brought closer to us when the news came through that the mother of Corporal Bennet, who was in charge of our MT section, had been killed by a flying bomb and he was sent home on compassionate leave.

We were as near to Paris as we were likely to get and it seemed a wonderful opportunity to give the lads a bit of recreation. The Army were still advancing rapidly and it appeared likely that we would not be long at La Vauraux, so I would have to move quickly. I told the adjutant to arrange for a three-tonner and to sort out a cross section of the unit to take part in a day trip. I got on to the GCC to find out if we were likely to move in the next twenty-four hours but had great difficulty in getting a decision. At last I got a reply from the chief controller himself that we were unlikely to be ordered to move in the next twenty-four hours. The liberty party who had been lucky enough to secure a place in the three-tonner had been waiting anxiously for a decision and immediately I got a ruling the vehicle was released and on its way in a flash.

The crowded three-tonner had left with the lads for their day trip to Paris. I had given them strict instructions as to the time of their return and I would have liked to have gone with them myself but knew that I should not and had sent the adjutant instead. The vehicle had not been gone more than fifteen minutes when I received a message that we were to move immediately to Melsbroek airfield in Brussels to act once again as a forward GCC. We would be reinforced by planning staff and extra R/T channels. I was astounded as I had only just cleared with GCC that we were not likely to move for twenty-four hours. I immediately sent out two airmen on motor cycles to chase after the three-tonner on different routes with orders to return after an hour if it could not be found. I had little hope that the motor cycles would be able to catch up with a three-tonner on its way to a unique chance to visit Paris. I was right, the vehicle could not be found. Short handed the rest of the unit dismantled all the equipment and the domestic site, loaded up as much as we could of the food, petrol, diesel and personal belongings and waited for the return of the liberty vehicle and the men. Fortunately the weather was excellent and it was possible for many of us to relax for a bit before starting the long drive to Brussels that would last through the night.

With the unit moving site so frequently there has been no mention of the amount of operational work being done by '054 and this can be shown by the unit diary entries for the short stay at La Vauroux between the 2nd and the 5th of September.

Sept 2   05.45 GCC contacted on (W/T) plotting channel, plotting
          commenced.
          10.25 Commenced controlling Front Line Patrols
              Potter a/c   4 Patrols
              Station a/c   4 Patrols
              Jamjar a/c   1 Armed Recce.
          17.40 No further a/c control plotting continues.
Sept 3   00.50 Crew stood down.
          07.15 Standing by for control.
          07.55 Commenced controlling Front Line Patrols
              Iceberg a/c   4 Patrols
              Wonder a/c   6 Patrols
              Friday a/c   2 Patrols
              Dauphin a/c   1 Patrol all uneventful
          20.40 Flying ceased
          23.40 Crew stood down. PBX open all night as a very
              busy message centre
Sept 4   06.30 Station operational
          08.00 Flying commenced no F.L.Ps.
              Armed Recce   Wolsey a/c
                            Jamjar a/c
                            Conrad a/c

          Station functioning as ops message centre.
          22.45 Night plotting
Sept 5   11.40 Instructed to close down radar and pack but PBX
              to be kept open until last minute.
          16.40 Unit packed GCC line linked to 122 Wing.

This was the log of the operations section of the unit which meant that the radar mechanics and fitters were equally employed as were the R/T and W/T communications sections. The domestic side would have been fully committed collecting rations and fuel or cooking meals or setting up domestic facilities. Just to ensure that we were all fully occupied there was the necessity to maintain what guards we could throughout the twenty-four hours when the RAF Regiment were not with us.

Chapter Eleven

The three-tonner returned from Paris as scheduled and those who had been on it were bursting to relate the wonders of their trip, whilst at the same time we that had been left behind were anxious to tell them our news. The Paris party was more than surprised to find that their tents and most of their personal baggage had already been packed for them and that we were waiting and raring to go. The returning vehicle was refuelled and loaded, the final briefing on drivers and routes given and we were on our way. It was to be a long trip to Brussels, over one hundred and fifty miles in convoy through the night. We were all tired already, either having been packing or else travelling to and from and around Paris. There was no chance of making it a fast trip as our big overloaded aerial vehicles were restricted to a maximum speed of twenty miles an hour for fear of the tires overheating and bursting.

Since the break-out from the bridge-head the unit had been either in the American Army zone or very close to it. Unlike the Army, we were not restricted on our choice of route or if we were we did not know and we chose to travel on the road that would take us through Bapaume, Cambrai, Valenciennes and Mons and which was in the First US Army zone. It turned out to be a good choice for the road was not crowded and the routes through the towns had been very clearly marked. We stopped at intervals to drink tea, eat, refuel and have a little rest. Night driving in convoy was a tiring business and we were tired before we started. Refuelling the vehicles in the dark was most difficult especially the Crossleys which only did about six miles to the gallon and whose filler nozzle was carefully designed to be almost inaccessible under the chassis floor. We did not have the benefit of the German jerricans and filler hoses then, our petrol came in rectangular shaped containers which carried four gallons. They were made from very thin soft metal sheet that was often accidentally punctured causing them to leak. To get the petrol out the tin had to be pierced at the top and pouring was very difficult. We had acquired a number of funnels and adapted some to cope with the awkwardly placed filler nozzles but a lot of fuel was spilled. I was leading the convoy in the jeep and found myself so tired that I nodded off several times as we ground steadily on our way.

In the middle of the night we were called to an emergency halt. The young officer of the 'Y' unit had driven his vehicle into a post marking the side of a railway crossing. Fortunately he had hit it so that the pole was dead central on his bonnet and neither his steering nor the vehicle lights were affected. The radiator had gone but his vehicle was able to be towed. Somewhere along the road in the early light we passed one of the great war cemeteries commemorating the 1914-18 war and the natural thought was 'here we go again'.

At last it became daylight which made driving easier and revived us somewhat. We crossed into Belgium and the change in the attitude of the people was most noticeable. Whereas in France we had met indifference and sometimes hostility, here small groups of people gathered at the side of the road and cheered us as we went by and held up bunches of flowers, quantities of apples and little gifts of eggs. We didn't stop however, that is I thought we did not stop, but I learned later that the last vehicle of our convoy took advantage of its position to make short stops and collect large quantities of the gifts and the kisses that were offered.

We were not far short of Brussels when we were brought to a halt. There were perhaps a couple of dozen Army vehicles ahead of us on the road and the word was passed back that we all had to wait for clearance before being allowed into the city. We waited and took advantage of the halt to wash and shave, enjoy a mug of tea and a sandwich provided by the cooks and to have a short rest.

It was not a long wait before we heard the sound of a small aircraft and an Auster circled and landed in a very small steep sided field beside the road. The message it brought was that we were cleared to enter Brussels. We remounted the vehicles and drove on again. As we drove through the outskirts of the city the cheering crowds increased and we were finally brought to a halt in the main square by the welcoming citizens who promptly climbed onto every vehicle giving happy greetings, hugs and kisses. The temptation was for us all to disappear for a couple of days to enjoy the celebrations just as, it was rumoured, the tank crews entering Paris had done. However, we had to get to Melsbroek and prepare for the arrival of the first fighter bomber squadrons. I enquired from someone the route to Melsbroek airfield, ordered the men back into their vehicles and we set off again.

We saw the deserted airfield on the right hand side of the road and carried on until we reached the main gate. As we drove the convoy on to the airfield very happy to have arrived at last we had the choice of the whole airfield for a site on which to set up the radar. Leaving the convoy parked just inside the entrance I drove quickly round most of the airfield in the jeep accompanied by Bill the Tech Officer, Hoppy and the adjutant. We noted the aircraft dispersal areas that had been used by the *Luftwaffe* and would obviously be wanted by the 83 Group squadrons when they arrived. We ignored the temptation to look at the few aircraft left by the Germans and decided to set up our equipment away from the flying area where there was a hangar that we could use for domestic vehicles and stores. We could sleep in the few available rooms and enjoy the ready built wash-basins and toilets that were still in working order.

We assembled the radar convoy and communications equipment once again and changed the interior of the ops vehicles so that we could display all the totes or information boards on squadron and airfield states and taskings that would be required in our role as forward GCC. Two planning Wing Commanders arrived to task the squadrons together with additional R/T vehicles. We modified our telephone switchboards to take the incoming telephone lines from the forward airfields as soon as they were laid by the ever efficient Air Formation Signals personnel, a selected few of the radar operator NCOs were chosen to act as deputy controllers when required. Whilst all this was going on the domestic vehicles were unloaded and the cooks prepared food in their now very efficient way.

The following day was a busy day for everyone coping with the workload of the Typhoon and Spitfire squadrons arriving at Melsbroek or the other airfields close by. The adjutant was working hard with his domestic team sorting out his supplies and domestic arrangements. The Army supply points for POL (fuel) and DID (food) did not materialize as promised, the weather turned cold and the wind whipped through the hangar. The throngs of local civilians who assembled to watch and enjoy every part of our domestic activities became an embarrassment making it necessary to place guards to keep them at a reasonable distance.

As soon as it was dark and air operations for the day had ceased, all those of us not on duty shot off into Brussels to enjoy a little of the welcome being extended so generously by the Belgians to the British troops. Every Belgian family was later to boast of 'our Englishman' proudly having adopted some serviceman or other. As I wandered through the streets of the city a young couple spoke to me and invited me to their home. They lived in a flat in the Rue Du Nord with their two very young children. Louis the husband told me that he had been in the

Belgian Army at the outbreak of war as an ajutant which I gathered was a form of officer cadet. His unit had been overrun by the Germans in 1940 and he had been taken prisoner and later released.

The number of 83 Group squadrons arriving on the local airfields increased steadily and we were very busy passing orders from the planning staff and providing listening watches on the R/T channels. It was to be our busiest time as we carried out the duties of a unit many times our size. The operations log recorded the following:

Sept 6		Arrived Melsbroek. Set up radar
Sept 7	05.30	Telephone line to 124 Wing working
	07.55	Telephone line to 143 Wing working
	08.30	Flying commenced
	09.25	First Front Line Patrol
	14.55	FLP recalled due to weather
	17.05	Telephone line to 126 Wing working
	21.10	Crew released to 0600
Sept 8	05.30	Radar operational
	06.37	Flying commenced. Now working 121, 122, 124, 125, 126, and 143 wings
	23.00	451 sorties flown today. No e/a seen, trains and barges attacked nr. Nijmegen
Sept 9	06.30	Radar operational
	06.45	Flying commenced
	20.45	Flying ceased. 360 sorties flown

All orders and messages between the planning team and the airfields came through us. All ground to air radio traffic and all logging of aircraft taking off and landing went through us. We were very busy.

On the second or third day at Melsbroek as I came out of the operations vehicle in the half light at the end of the day I noticed that there was some activity with a couple of military vehicles not far away from our convoy. I walked across and saw to my surprise that a Light Warning radar was being set up. The signs on the vehicle showed that it belonged to 85 Base Defence Group that controlled the Mosquito night fighters.

The Light Warning radars were very inferior compared with our equipment having a small display console, limited range and vertical coverage and no height finding capability. I got into conversation with an officer standing about in a raincoat with no rank markings and he confirmed that it was intended that Mosquito night fighters for the defence of the Brussels area would be controlled on the Light Warning radar. I pointed to our convoy with its advantages of better plan radars, height finding equipment and more powerful R/T channels and invited him to use it. To my great astonishment my offer was refused. I talked of all the advantages but the offer was again declined and I decided that 85 Group was intent on fighting its own private war. I learned later that the officer concerned was the head of 85 Group operations. The work load increased and we now had squadrons from four airfields under our control. We were getting little sleep having continued to visit Brussels after dark and starting operations each day at six o'clock in the morning.

I had been invited to a 'Liberation' party at the flat of Louis and Paulette who had first entertained me on my arrival in Brussels. I asked Mac the Canadian Squadron Leader from Group who had just arrived in Brussels to accompany me. It was an enjoyable noisy party limited a bit for us since Mac's French was almost non-existent and I was still recalling my schoolday French lessons. There had been some joking about the prudish attitudes of the British and how we were embarrassed at their talk of their little Brussels boy of whom they were so proud. I was vastly intrigued after that to hear in a temporary quiet in the men's group a shrill female voice shouting, 'Deux fois par mois, je vous demandes ce n'est pas assis,' and loud laughter followed. The noisiest laughter was yet to come. Mac came over to me and whispered that he was dying for a pee. I called our hostess Paulette over and asked if Mac could wash his hands. She beckoned him to follow her and took him into the bathroom where there was a bath, a wash-basin, a bidet and a chest of drawers. (The WC was in a separate room.) Mac stood there looking rather foolish and Paulette in her limited English said, "Carry on do not be embarrassed," and turned to the chest of drawers to find him a towel. Mac was by now fairly desperate and proceeded to unbutton his flies prepared to use the bidet. Fortunately Paulette turned round at that moment and seeing what was happening rushed back into the general party shrieking with laughter and anxious to relate the story.

We had operated as a forward GCC continuously for four days when the forward elements of the GCC arrived and I was called for by the Group Captain. He thanked me for the efforts of '054 and asked that I continue to keep the unit hard on the heels of the forward units of the Army as it advanced. I took the opportunity to press for '054 to have a well earned forty-eight hour rest in Brussels. To my great disappointment the Group Captain gave a very definitive 'No' saying, "John, I must have my forward radar cover."

We therefore pushed on to a site at Velpen just outside Louvain moving in two echelons in order to get continuous radar control cover by setting up the Type 15 and R/T on the new forward site before closing down the site at Melsbroek. It was at Velpen on a foggy night that there was an accident when a sentry from the military guard that we had been given fired a shot and discovered that the man he had shot was another member of the guard. LAC MacDonald our medical orderly gave the man first aid and we rushed him to hospital on a stretcher fixed on the top of the jeep but heard that he had died later. The Army advance had slowed considerably and we were waiting impatiently to hear when we would be able to make another forward leap.

Word had come through that the Army had crossed the Albert Canal at Beringen and Mac came along again for a siting trip to see how far we could move forward. Bill and I went with him in the jeep and we managed to get across the canal but the situation was hopeless. It was obvious that the Army had not got much of a bridge-head and the two streets that they had were full of guns and mortars. There was no sign of any likely site for the radar. We returned back across the bridge and decided to try the area further to the north. We found ourselves on a long straight tree lined road heading roughly east but the area there was also unsuitable as a radar site. Mac suggested that we tried turning off right but that was rising ground and wooded and obviously still not suitable and I spoke against it. Suddenly there was a sharp crack, I asked the others what they thought it was as it sounded to me like a rifle shot. Mac said, "Just a twig under the wheels I expect." We then saw a small group of houses on our left set well back from the road. The nearest building was a café/bar and there were about eight local civilians leaning against the outside and talking. We stopped the jeep but the men made no move. I got out and walked towards them asking, "Does anyone speak French?" One of the men came towards me and I asked him, "Where is everyone?" I meant of course that I wanted to know where our Army was, but he said to me, "If you want the Germans there are twenty of them in the cellar of the second house up there," and pointed to the few houses behind and to the right of the café. I thanked him for the information and walked smartly back to the jeep. We lost no time turning round and driving at a good speed back to the nearest village.

We stopped outside the first café and went in and ordered three blond beers. The woman smiled and served us with our beer for which I tendered some money but the woman declined it. I thought she objected to the new military currency and explained that it was legal tender, but she would not take the money and I assumed she was being generous to us as we were British. Just as we started to drink our beer there was the ding of the shop bell and the door opened and in walked two British soldiers. They said nothing but we watched fascinated at their subsequent actions. The leading man put his hand into his pocket and took out a packet of cigarettes. The hand holding the packet was shaking so badly that he had difficulty grabbing it with the other hand, opening the packet, getting out a cigarette and with his hand shaking violently getting the cigarette into his mouth. He then offered the packet to his mate with the hand still shaking violently.

The actions of the men were very puzzling so I said, "What is wrong with you two, then?" The leading one then repeated several times in a shaky voice "Never been so frightened in me life, never been so frightened in me life." It transpired that the two men were driver and co-driver of a large truck carrying petrol destined for an Army Brigade HQ. They must have gone off route as they found themselves facing a blown bridge over a canal. As they stopped and went to reverse their vehicle, a machine-gun from the other side of the canal opened up on them. In their panic they got their vehicle stuck in the ditch and had to get out and run for it. They had made their way to the village and were looking for the nearest Army unit. We offered to take them in our jeep and they were very grateful. After driving a couple of miles we came across an Army unit which was apparently the same Brigade HQ that should have received the petrol and we told the story to a major in the operations section who said he would send a tank around to clear up the situation. I was surprised to learn that the Army often just drove through an area and if there was no opposition that was it . . . captured or liberated territory and no troops were left there.

It was the 20th of September just fourteen days after we had arrived in Brussels that I went off with Bill the signals officer and an officer from GCC to explore the country towards Bree that looked promising as a site. There was an area on the map that was marked as an old artillery range that we wanted to look at. Having driven around for a while we came across a small café at a lonely crossroads and went in to have a beer. A very pleasant young woman came to the counter, smiled at us and said, "F . . . me gently." We were speechless at receiving such an instruction or request on so short an acquaintanceship and at such an hour of the day. We gave her friendly smiles, ignored her request and ordered some beer. Discussing the situation as we drank our beer we came to the conclusion that some British soldier with an odd sense of humour had taught the girl that it was a normal English greeting, like 'Hello', or 'Good-day'. We decided that it would be in the best interests of Anglo/Belgian relations if we tactfully persuaded her to change her greeting to words that were a little less intimate.

We drove eastwards on a road that skirted the northern edge of the area marked as an artillery range and as we got towards the far end we saw a large German Wurtzburg radar aerial leaning at a drunken angle on its concrete mounting. We drove in at a barred entrance and found an abandoned German radar site. The equipment had been blown up and the wooden huts badly damaged with all windows, electric lights and fitments broken, but we decided it would make an ideal site for us. It was named Wanberg but was known to most of us as Meeuwen which was the name of the little village near by. We arrived there with the convoy the next day and started to make ourselves comfortable, the cooks getting to work in the lightly damaged kitchen right away. It was getting late in the year and living under canvas was beginning to be less enjoyable, and as if to emphasize this the weather changed for the worse. We were very happy to be in the huts and set about making them waterproof and comfortable as quickly as possible.

The Germans could not have been long gone, as I found two civilians rummaging around the site looking for anything worth picking up. I yelled at them to go away and waved my arms to indicate that they should leave the site which they appeared to do, but a short while after I came upon them again. I was furious and drew my revolver and fired two shots into the ground. The men immediately ran off at an excellent pace and scrambled quickly over the boundary security wire and still kept on running. We had no further trouble of that kind.

The site was excellent technically and the more we looked around the better it seemed domestically. There were defence trenches lined with fir poles that had been dug by the Germans and a fine covered area which would accommodate our vehicles and enable us to do some much needed maintenance especially on the GP three-tonners that had put up such a lot of miles collecting fuel and rations and so on. The diesels had been running continuously and were also in urgent need of attention.

We normally did minor maintenance of vehicles and diesels ourselves whilst other maintenance and repair was done by the Group MTLRU (MT Light Repair Unit). However, as a forward signals unit we were extremely vulnerable to any breakdown or accident, the loss of a single vehicle could put the whole unit out of action. Repairs by the

90

MTLRU were often impracticable as that unit was generally back in the rear areas and any vehicle sent to it was gone for some time if not for ever. Because of this we often used the Royal Engineers' roadside workshops which were very efficient and helpful and with a little encouragement would change a half shaft for us with no trouble at all.

It may not have been in accordance with Group Orders but we found that there were many of these with which we could not comply and keep operating. What could I do to comply with the ruling, 'All drivers and co-drivers shall after a unit move be given twenty-four hours free of all duties'? We had a basic personnel strength of about fifty and half that number of vehicles. Who would do the technical duties, the domestic duties, the guards?

The unit was working well, everyone sharing equally and each knowing that we were doing more than our share in helping win the war.

Chapter Twelve

We had only been four days on the site at Meeuwen but we were settling in nicely and some of the unit had been organizing beer supplies and others preparing to put on a concert for our entertainment. Early in the morning (25th Sept) at watch changeover time, one of the cipher sergeants came to me with an 'IMMEDIATE' signal that had come in on the W/T link and which he had just decoded. The signal ordered us to move our 'B' echelon at once on Second Army authority to a given pin-point for 'defensive fighter control duties'. The signal also stated that we would be provided with a military escort which would arrive at 11.00 hours. We looked up the pin-point on the map and found to our astonishment that it was in the sea between some of the Dutch Islands. However, we had all been following the BBC news of the airborne landings at Arnhem over the past week and by changing the letters of the map reference squares the signal made more sense.

We did not understand the 'B' echelon bit but then realized that it was the reference given to our main party that landed in Normandy on D plus 5. We at once set about the job of deciding what equipment, personnel and admin support to take. There was no fat on the unit when running as a single entity let alone as two. The most reasonable solution was to take the Type 11 plan radar and the Type 13 heightfinder together with the R/T vehicles, W/T and cooking facilities. We also decided to take twenty-four of the RAF Regiment flight that was with us for guard duties. We needed fuel for the MT, for the diesels and food for ourselves, all for an unknown period. A basic movement order was therefore produced on those lines. Bill and Hoppy would come with me leaving Monty and the adjutant with the Type 15 to run the rest of the unit which we would leave behind.

Everyone was called together and briefed on the situation. We were to move to the Grave area near Nijmegen to provide radar coverage and control of fighters in defence of the bridges. Since 2nd Army had asked specially for us and was supplying an escort then I assumed we had priority over all other traffic on the roads. No one was to stop or allow his vehicle to be diverted. When the list of people chosen to go to Grave was read out I cannot remember anyone asking to be left behind.

Squadron Leader MacGregor the Group Radar (Operations) Staff Officer turned up at the unit and in view of the various uncertainties about the whole business I went off with him to 83 Group Main headquarters for clarification and to get the essential Second Army priority movement document that we would need to get through, we left the rest of the unit to pack and get on the road. At the Group Head-quarters I was told that heavy *Luftwaffe* attacks were anticipated against the Nijmegen area and 15054 was to control standing fighter patrols that were to be set up using the fifteen fighter squadrons that were part of 83 Group. We were not on any account to direct the fighters away from the area presumably because the sight and sound of the RAF overhead would keep up the Army's morale, although I suspected the real reason was the usual lack of faith in radar and ground control.

The fighters to be used in the defence role were 125, 126, and 127 Wings equipped with Spitfire IXs and 122 Wing with Mustang IIIs. All were flying from airfields around Brussels which were about a hundred miles from Nijmegen, whilst the Germans had the advantage of being able to launch their attacks from home airfields that were much nearer. Both 126 and 127 Wings were RCAF Wings consisting of Squadrons Nos. 401, 411, 412, 442 and 403, 416, 421, 443 respectively. 125 Wing had two RCAF Squadrons Nos 441 and 453 in addition to 132 and 602. The Mustang Squadrons of 122 Wing were Nos. 19, 65 and 122.

Generally we did not know the squadrons by their number but by their R/T callsigns Potter, Station, Jamjar, Iceberg or Wonder and so on. We answered with our call-sign of Bazar but we did not know the pilots nor they us, they did not know of the capabilities of our radar or that we had one, we were just a control voice on the radio. I just hoped always that the orders and information that I gave over the radio had enough ring of confidence for the pilots to believe in what I was telling them. Their lives could depend on it.

Getting the convoy ready was more difficult than usual. The problem was the selection, sorting and packing of the limited number of support vehicles with food, fuel and spares that we might need. The diesel power generators would certainly require a lot of fuel and we might need enough food for a week or so as it was unlikely that we would be able to call on Army supply depots for some time. We set about dismantling the radar, the R/T and communications equipment, but with everyone giving a hand we were ready long before the time the Army escort was due. When

93

the escort arrived we were surprised and a bit deflated to find it was no more than a single despatch rider with the 30 Corps white boar insignia on his motor cycle. However, we bore the Second Army authority and we were confident that that, together with the odd appearance of our out-of-gauge aerial vehicles would give us an air of importance sufficient to get us through.

Grave was only about fifty miles due north when measured directly on the map but we had to drive due west at first, then north-east to pick up the route of the narrow thrust made by the Army towards Arnhem. We set out at what was for our vehicles a good pace hoping to make Grave which would be about one hundred miles by road before dark. We made good time and crossed into Holland, very surprised to see that the border was marked only by a small wooden barrier. It was only a few miles further on that our troubles began when we came across a line of Army trucks parked at the side of the road. The drivers were out of their vehicles and were brewing up tea and eating their rations out of tins in the odd way the Army had. This forced our vehicles on to the far side of the narrow road and the pace slowed. The number of parked trucks became greater, there were trucks with food, ammunition and petrol. In front of them further on were vast numbers of guns with their towing vehicles and then tanks parked end to end. At one halt we got out and saw to our surprise a coach full of ENSA girls bound for Eindhoven so they said.

The Army jeered good naturedly at the sight of our oddshaped aerial vehicles and our canvas and cardboard covered convoy vehicles. When we told them of our intention of getting through the traffic some tank drivers said they had not been able to move for two whole days. Various attempts were made to stop us but we pressed steadily on. LAC Coogan a driver by trade, driving one of the leading aerial vehicles gained a momentous victory in a well voiced debate with a full brigadier. Finally our luck seemed to run out. The whole convoy was brought to a halt by a large truculent military policeman who blocked the road. The MP produced a fluent flow of invective against our presence in that part of the world, on that route, on the wrong side of the road and so on. During a pause whilst he drew breath for a further onslaught the Second Army authority was produced with a flourish! This brought an immediate change in the situation. We were assured that the way would be cleared for us at once! We remounted our vehicles and started up again. The road *was* cleared for us as if by magic. In triumph we passed more tanks and vehicles parked endlessly on the roadside. Signs of heavy fighting that had taken place were everywhere, but in less than an hour on a sunny afternoon we entered the town of Eindhoven that was empty of military traffic.

It was good to see the orange coloured national flags flying everywhere and to receive smiles and waves from the townspeople. At the first main crossroads I was surprised to see a uniformed figure dressed wholly in black with polished jackboots directing the traffic. I remarked to my co-driver that the SS seemed still to be in the town. We both had a good laugh but I was a bit embarrassed when the man in uniform leant across the jeep as we went by and asked in perfect English, "What is so amusing?" We were directed by our Army escort to park in one of the town's main streets and were soon surrounded by an interested crowd of children and adults. It appeared that there was a hold up on the road running north from the town, but we had no immediate news although we could see Typhoon aircraft diving on targets not far away.

We began our long wait. At five o'clock the cook produced a brew of tea and we ate cold corned beef and the standby biscuits of the compo rations. The temperature started to fall and we all felt cold, tired and dirty. Some of the men had shared their meal and sweets with the children that were hanging about but they had now disappeared off home. We had been told that the town had been bombed two days previously causing many casualties and as a result no Army convoys were allowed to stay overnight in the town! We were alone. The only news we could get was that the road to the north had been cut by the Germans and many vehicles had been destroyed. We stood around a bit more but there was still no sign of any move. Finally we gave up all hope of being able to move off that night and settled down to a cold and uncomfortable night in the vehicle driving cabs.

Up early next morning we washed and breakfasted and prepared to move immediately we had the word. The news was passed to us that the original road was still closed but the Army had erected a bridge over a canal on a minor road to the north-east and we would be the first convoy across and up the new route. We waited a while and were then marshalled and moved off steadily behind a group of recce Bren-gun carriers only to be stopped in a narrow lane and directed to park closely at the side under overhanging trees. No information was passed to us and as the minutes went by I felt more and more nervous. An Army NCO then came along and told us the bridge was not far away and it was almost complete, they were just levelling off the approaches to it for us. After a short wait we were off again and suddenly as we rounded a bend we saw the Bailey

95

bridge over a canal ahead of us and we carefully drove each vehicle across it.

We followed close behind the Bren-gun carriers that advanced slowly up the road. There were no other troops to be seen and the situation seemed a bit unreal. It was some time before we met up with the original main road running up to Nijmegen and to our relief found ourselves with more of the Army. We saw a long line of burnt out British supply trucks that had been caught by the enemy, it was a sharp reminder of the danger we were in. There were now numbers of American troops lining the route which puzzled us as we did not know then of the great part the 82nd and 101st U.S. divisions had played in the airborne landings.

Arriving at last at the pin-point near Grave that we had been given we found a suitable site close to the railway bridge over the Maas and set up the radar and communications equipment and pitched the tents. The site had a clear view to the east round to south from where we expected the enemy aircraft to come. LAC Scales our most experienced motor cyclist and convoy escort had disappeared somewhere on the road. To our great relief he turned up fit and well. He had misread his map and lost his way. He found two Army types in a slit trench and when he stopped to check his location they warned him not to go further down that road as the uniforms there changed colour!

We were unable to make contact with the GCC by W/T but over the R/T we received a message from Kenway (GCC) via an aircraft that we were to pass information to the fighters. It was now late in the day and the fighters were on their way home to their airfield near Brussels. We had no contact with any Army unit and had no idea what the ground situation was, it got dark and very chilly. There was nothing to do but to mount our RAF Regiment guards, have a mug of hot soup and retire to bed ready for what we hoped would be a successful day on the morrow. I arranged that we would be fully manned at first light.

I undressed before going to bed and folded my uniform and laid it on top of the bed. I woke up once or twice during the night feeling very cold and was pleased when the guard gave me a call in the morning. I reached for my clothes and was astonished to find them stiff and very wet with the heavy dew. There was no alternative but to put on my damp uniform and go on watch. We were all very excited hoping that we would have plenty of opportunities to intercept enemy aircraft. I had been briefed that I was on no account to direct the standing fighter patrols away from the bridge-head but I felt sure that as I passed the first information on approaching enemy aircraft the defensive fighters would naturally turn towards them, I would then be able to pass clock codes and distances and relative heights to the fighters as they emerged from the ground clutter and would be seen clearly on the radar.

The radar was serviceable, that is both the Type 11 search radar and the Type 13 height finder. The R/T was serviceable too and we were listening out eagerly waiting for the appearance of the first defensive patrol. Our first squadrons of fighter aircraft appeared from the south-west and took up position for their patrol line. I gave the leader a call using our own call-sign and asked him to relay a message to GCC (Kenway) that we would pass information to all defensive fighters.

The fighter patrol had been going up and down for some time before the first enemy raid of the day was picked up by the radar at about seventy miles to the south-east. The radar response was large enough for it to be several aircraft. I passed the initial information to the fighter leader of the presence of the enemy aircraft, the bearing and distance, estimated number and estimated height. The Type 13 heightfinder operator turned the aerial to nod in the direction of the raid. Its pick-up range was always less than that of the plan radar. As I expected the formation leader called his aircraft together and the fighters turned towards the enemy leaving the ground clutter so that I could now see clearly both the fighter and enemy formations on the radar.

This meant that I was then able to give the fighter leader the exact ranges of the enemy aircraft from him and their position as a clock code so that he could concentrate his attention in that direction. One of the senior NCOs had taken over the job as Type 13 height operator and read off the enemy height in thousands of feet, but as the raid came closer a relative height between our fighters and the enemy could easily be seen and this information was more accurate and helped focus the pilots' attention. Calling off the clock code or bearing of the enemy from our fighters and the distance and height difference as the two formations closed soon brought a sighting of the enemy and the R/T was then full of pilots leaders giving instructions or others calling warnings and then the curses and the yells of success that go with any air battle.

No sooner had that enemy formation been repulsed and our fighters been relieved by the next squadrons of fighters than we picked up another incoming enemy formation. The heights were unexpectedly low, below twenty thousand feet probably because the enemy airfields were not far away from the Nijmegen bridge-head. Everyone of the crew was excited as this was the air defence interception work that we had looked forward to for so long. We had expected that the Normandy landing would have been opposed by large formations of the *Luftwaffe* but the raids there had been relatively few in number and spread over a long time period.

The control of the standing patrols of fighters was always much the same but the excitement and tension was ever present. The controller sat immediately in front of the PPI display with his R/T headset on watching constantly the radar trace rotating four times every minute. An NCO operator or senior airman manned the Type 13 heightfinder display alongside sitting in front of it watching the trace nodding up and down. Between the two and close behind sat the raid teller who normally manned the plotting line to the GCC. The watch NCO kept the log of events and the dead reckoning tracker listened in on the plotting line and used the plots for his records and raid speed and course calculations. The position of the fighters was followed on the radar but it became difficult or impossible when the fighters were patrolling near to the radar site because of the ground clutter or responses from nearby high ground.

The time between picking up the incoming enemy formations and their interception probably took no more than ten minutes. The first indication of an enemy raid would be a brightening of the trace at some distant point. Was it an aircraft or just noise or interference? A slight mark with chinagraph pencil on the PPI and an even more careful watch as the trace came round to that direction on its next sweep. A pointed finger and a remark 'New track' to inform the heightfinder operator and the teller. Quite unnecessary of course as they were equally observant. A call to the fighter leader on the R/T.

"Station Leader I have Bandits to the south-east at range 70."

"Roger, Bazar." That was our call-sign but he was equally likely to have said "Roger, Kenway" as all ground control was usually accepted as coming from Kenway, which was the GCC call-sign.

The heightfinder operator meanwhile will have turned his aerial round to nod in the direction of the incoming raid. The aerial direction showed as a white trace on the PPI that turned to coincide with the direction in which the Type 13 aerial pointed. I passed the range of the raid from the station so that the operator could concentrate on that section of his display to look for a response. It was time to pass further information to the fighters. By now I would have an idea of the raid height from our radar pick up range, I could estimate the number of aircraft from the response and could see that the echoes were moving towards us.

"Station Leader twenty plus Bandits estimated at Angels twenty."

"Roger."

"Bandits now range 60 heading north-west towards you."

"Roger." The fighters could be seen leaving the ground clutter of the radar as they headed towards the incoming raid. The fighter leader would have a few words to his formation on tactics or formation. It was time to concentrate on the height of the raid. The heightfinder operator inched the Type 13 aerial a couple of degrees or so across the direction of the raid hoping to increase his chances of picking it up. There was a response . . . it showed a height of twenty thousand feet.

"Station Leader confirm Bandits at Angels twenty, range now 45."

It was time for the controller himself to cast an eye at the heightfinder responses hoping to see the enemy raid pattern, e.g. if the aircraft were flying at different levels and how many there appeared to be. Could the fighters be picked up so that the relative heights can be seen? It was time for more information to the fighters.

"Bandits heading 330 now at half-past eleven range 30."

"Roger."

"Bandits are three thousand below now estimate thirty plus."

"Roger, three thousand below."

"Bandits moving to eleven o'clock range 18."

"Roger."

"Station Leader Bandits now eleven o'clock range 12."

"Roger."

"Station Leader, Bandits now at eleven o'clock three thousand below range six." There is a call from one of the squadron of a sighting of the enemy. The leader confirms that he can see them too. There is nothing more we can do now. It is all up to the skill of the pilots as to how the battle goes. We just hope that our information has given them an initial tactical advantage.

So the whole day continued with enemy formations coming from both the Ruhr airfield complex and the Rheine airfields and a succession of defending fighter formations replacing each other. We, the crew of '054 were all happy and confident knowing that we were giving the defending fighters the best of information and what is more we inter-cepted every incoming formation. As it got dusk so we picked up a number of single aircraft coming in which I reported to the formation leader. He was most apologetic saying that he could not stay as he had to leave in order to be back at his airfield to land in daylight. We watched the enemy aircraft come in and there were no night fighters to be seen opposing them. I thought of all the long months that I had spent in the

99

UK waiting in vain for enemy activity and only able to carry out practice interceptions with our night fighters. We now had regretfully lots of enemy activity and no night fighters to control and no information on any night fighter R/T frequencies which might be used.

It had been a wonderfully successful day as far as we were concerned, we had been busy all day. The quiet confidence of the fighter leaders had impressed me very much. When I gave an initial warning of fifty plus German aircraft the Wing Leader just said, "All right boys, get together," and I felt the ring of leadership that anyone would follow. With the accurate and up to date information off the radar being passed directly to the pilots and the experience of the fighter leaders it was all so different from the air battles of 1940.

By the time we left the operations vehicle it was already dark and very cold and damp. There was nothing to do but have an early supper of hot soup and so to bed at 19.45 leaving the RAF Regiment guards to protect us. I took good care to put my uniform in the bed with me to protect it from the dew. After another cold and uncomfortable night we were up again early ready for work.

The air defence against the raiding German aircraft went on much as before but on a smaller scale. The previous day was to be the Germans greatest effort when raids of about 600 aircraft attempted to attack the Nijmegen Bridge and the fighters had claimed to have destroyed 46 of them.

We were surprised when a 'W' unit arrived unannounced. It was a small ground to ground R/T unit which when set up put us in speech contact with the GCC forward element and we were then able to pass plots on the air picture and also let them know what was going on. We had been having trouble maintaining contact on the W/T link, but speech contact with the GCC was to be a mixed blessing. After another busy day and no contact with local Army units we again went off to an early bed.

In the night I was wakened by the guards who reported firing close by. I quickly dressed and went outside where I was astonished to see a considerable amount of small arms tracer fire travelling horizontally in opposing directions not far away. It all looked very dangerous but as we had no contact with any other unit in the area and no defensive positions the best action to take seemed to be to ignore it and draw no attention to ourselves. I told the guards to call me of things looked any more dangerous and went back to bed not knowing what else to do. We were not to know it then but the firing was probably associated with the specially trained German troops that swam down the Rhine rivers that night and attacked the road and rail bridges over the rivers with some success.

The following day the 29th we were controlling as usual when a message came over the plotting line that we were to cease controlling and just continue to pass plots on the incoming raids! I was unable to believe the message and asked for it to be repeated. It was incredible that after all the successes against the *Luftwaffe* raids using the immediate radar picture and the height finder information that it was all to be thrown away for someone else to control on inferior information. We were perfectly sited and had intercepted every incoming raid. What could better our performance? I was furious and resentful. The rest of the unit naturally took its mood from me and I knew the situation had to be resolved quickly.

I sat it out for the rest of what had been a black day and decided that whatever the ground situation was I had to go back to Eindhoven and find out what was going on. The situation on the roads was still not good. Flight Sergeant White our senior radar fitter had tried to reach us with some radar spares and NAAFI rations but the vehicle in front of him had been hit by a German shell and he rightly decided to exercise a bit of discretion and turned back. The road north of Eindhoven was cut several times by the Germans after we first travelled up it.

Early the next day I drove off to find the forward GCC somewhere near Eindhoven. To my surprise I saw the 15053 convoy and concluded quite wrongly that '053 had somehow arranged to do all the controlling. I went in to find Millbank the CO and demanded most forcibly to know what was going on. Millbank put his hand in the air as if to pacify me and said, "John, I had nothing to do with it. How do you think I feel? I am not allowed to do any controlling either and they are using my plots in a lean-to tent against my own vehicles! I need sympathy too."

I found the lean-to tent as Millbank had said, inside it a small map board was being used as a general situations map with two airmen plotting the raids being passed by 15053 and '054. There was a sergeant deputy controller operating the R/T and a junior officer acting as the Raid Recognition officer. I went in to the GCC Wing Commander and asked why we had suddenly been forbidden to control the standing patrols over Nijmegen Bridge?

I was told that we did not have the 'Broad Picture'. I asked what that was seeing that the fighters were defending a single point. The answer to this was that only the GCC through its Raid Recognition could decide which tracks were hostile. I pointed out that we could see the German aircraft forming up over the Rheine airfield complex and also the Ruhr airfield complex prior to their coming in, but this comment was ignored. I explained that I was a trained radar controller, that I had immediate access to up-to-date radar information of position together with relative and actual heights of all the aircraft. I was told none of that was necessary and that they, the forward GCC would do the controlling from the tiny plotting table.

The anti-radar school I thought held all the tricks and it looked as though I was completely outplayed. I produced my last card. I said that I was not satisfied that the GCC control on old inaccurate information was the best and that if any of the defensive fighter patrols were jumped and lost pilots I would be forced to express my opinion. This produced the reaction that I hoped for . . . "Well, if there is an incident in which it looks as though our aircraft are at risk then you may pass your warning." It was enough. I knew that I could go back and carry on passing our information to the fighters. I had no need to use the '054 call-sign (Bazar) and I knew that the deputy controller at the GCC would hardly be likely to say that anyone else had been operating.

Morale at our '054 site had been very low since the orders to cease transmissions had come in. The main unit function was to carry out successful interceptions of enemy aircraft. At Nijmegen our great chance that we had dreamed of had come. On the first day of our controlling not a single formation had gone unintercepted and forty-six aircraft had been claimed by the fighters as destroyed, the same interception success on the second day with claims of eleven. To have been stopped controlling after that had been a nasty shock to us all. However, we were now back in business ready for anything that the *Luftwaffe* might do.

The *Luftwaffe* tactics suddenly changed when on the 1st October we saw not mass raids by normal propeller driven aircraft, but the first of the jets. They came in singly, easily recognized by the distance they covered in one sweep, that is the fifteen seconds of one rotation of the radar aerial. The fighter patrols were warned of the incoming jets and on the 2nd October reported many sightings. The next day the weather was poor and there was little activity but on the 4th there were again many sightings of the jets but no combats.

I took an opportunity to slip into Nijmegen to see what the Army ground situation was like and to my astonishment saw signs for recreation clubs and bath units. It seemed hard to reconcile them with the fact that the single road north of Eindhoven had been cut several times and that as a result tanks and vast numbers of supply vehicles were unable to move north. Back at the site there was the sound of low flying aircraft and a formation of fifty Dakotas appeared and as they turned they went into line astern coming down to land at the nearby airfield at Grave. Just as the last was about to land so another formation of fifty appeared to be followed by yet another fifty. It seemed lucky that the Army did not have to rely on supplies brought up by road.

The 5th October started quietly with the usual fighter patrols, no enemy activity until afternoon when just on three o'clock a formation of thirty plus enemy aircraft and a jet came in almost simultaneously. Blackout Squadron (401) claiming a jet aircraft (Me 262) shared by Sqn. Ldr. Smith and four others. The aircraft burned and crashed and was claimed as the first German jet to be destroyed by the RAF and RCAF. Kapok Squadron (403) claimed five Me 109s from the raiding formation. There were more single raids by jet aircraft. The next day the 6th October was similar as there was no enemy activity until the afternoon at 15.30 when Station and Kapok squadrons were on patrol and a formation of 50 plus hostiles came in. There was a great combat with ten enemy aircraft claimed as destroyed.

That was the last big raid as far as we were concerned. Early next morning the German jet aircraft came in and we intercepted them but there were no claims. GCC continued to query our plotting, wanting to know how we knew they were jet aircraft. We had no problem recognizing the tracks as the echoes seemed to leap along on each rotation of the aerial. One was tempted to give GCC a facetious answer saying that the jet echoes had a hole in them where the propellers were missing but they would not have understood. In the afternoon we received instructions to close down and return to our main site at Meewen. We packed up and left at 09.00 the next day.

It had been a wonderful experience. We had helped to beat off the biggest sustained *Luftwaffe* attacks on the British Sector. We had controlled the defensive Spitfire and Mustang squadrons so that they were able to intercept all the enemy formations and we knew we had done well. We had been at risk and we had had no casualties. The GCC never passed a word of praise or of thanks to us but we were content.

By the time we returned to the Meeuwen site from Grave we were all very tired. Since leaving our first site in Normandy we had made ten moves in about sixty days and to add to the stress of packing and unpacking and all the driving there was always the possibility of enemy action against us. At Meeuwen we were only about five miles from the front line but it was a quiet area and we did not feel under threat. We settled down to making our stay as pleasant as possible, the weather was worsening and it did not seem that we would move far for some time.

A mobile detachment of the Group MTLRU (Motor Transport Light Repair Unit) honoured us with a six day visit and went to work on our transport, after which all having been cleaned the vehicles looked and sounded very much healthier. We had been blessed with very little trouble from our MT vehicles which were so essential to our working.

There had been a bit of excitement for those who did not go to Grave when a Typhoon of 257 Squadron in 84 Group forced landed on the site because of engine failure. It only just missed the airmen's barrack block and fortunately the pilot was unhurt as well. Group Headquarters must have decided none of us would be moving for some time as they issued an order that we were to go back into blue uniform again with effect 31 October. We had patched the huts up so that they were now waterproof and we had got the heating stoves into working order. Operationally we were working steadily on a twenty-four hour basis. By day there were usually a few fighter patrols to control up and down the border to counter any low flying raids, but we never picked up any on the radar nor were there any ground reports of raids. One day there was a thunderous roar and I thought a Squadron of P47 Thunderbolts was approaching but it was only a single V-1 that flew over at very low level. I assume it must have been off course as we were not on their normal lines of flight.

Just down the road a couple of miles or so was an 85 Group (Base Defence) GCI whose duty it was to intercept the enemy night raiders. All the unit personnel were living in tents and they had been forced to move them more than once in the autumn when the mud got too deep.

How the unit managed during the cold winter I do not know. As far as I was concerned they could all have gone home as we would have been delighted to have carried out their night fighter control duties for them.

We were only about sixty miles east of Brussels and it was possible to arrange passes and short leave for everyone and generally transport too. It was a great treat as the unit had lived since its formation well away from towns and the bright lights. In Brussels, cinemas, clubs and dances were available together with the chance of meeting Belgian civilians as well as other British troops. At Meeuwen football was the main recreation and we played with any other Army or RAF unit which could find a team. The lads were quite keen and our team was well run by two of the junior NCOs who felt they had as good a side as any in the area.

There were those who claimed that they were an authority on the local beer and having tried a number of breweries the unit's favourite tipple was a beer produced in one of the local monasteries. It had a heavy red colour and good strength. The Group Captain from GCC paid us another visit as did a few staff officers, including two from the UK, Squadron Leader Longstaffe of Radar Records of Air Ministry and Squadron Leader Pool from 60 Group.

There was a good talking point one day which was to be referred to frequently, when one of the radar mechanics working on the diesels attempted to walk across from one diesel platform to the other and got stuck with electricity running up one leg and down the other. Fortunately he came to no real harm but was thereafter known as 'The Man They Could Not Kill'.

The food had changed for the better. We were no longer living on Compo rations but on fresh food stocks, captured from the Germans it was said. The meat seemed to be of very low quality and the general opinion was that the Germans had been swindled. However, everyone appreciated having fresh bread and the cooks were doing a good job with the rations and also providing extra tea and rations for those on the 'night bind'. Those in Corporal Gallops's favour could count on getting hot water for shaving too.

The job of cook on a small very mobile unit such as 15054 was not an enviable one and there was a well-known story that went the rounds. It appears that on a similar but smaller radar unit in the desert in N. Africa the unit cook went sick and there being no one willing to volunteer to act as cook the CO detailed one man for the job with the proviso that the first airman to complain would be required to take over the job. Time went on and no one complained so the stand-in cook let the meals deteriorate but in spite of his efforts no airman made audible complaint. The temporary cook decided that desperate measures were called for and carefully arranged on one of the meal servings a little camel dung. The unfortunate airman who received the doctored meal started to eat it and then suddenly realizing what he was eating leapt to his feet with a shout, "My God, camel shit." His face suddenly crumpled as he realized what he had said and the immediate disaster that faced him. His brain worked swiftly and he quickly added, "But, mark you, nicely cooked."

It is difficult to select people for special mention in a unit that is running well. Each NCO in charge of his own section kept it running smoothly and each section integrated into the whole unit both through Sergeant Poulter the sergeant disciplinarian and through operational working. Not everyone was brilliant of course but all were willing and the unit had been together long enough for each person to be employed to his best according to his abilities and interests.

There were those who ran their own little empire such as Cpl. Lindley who looked after all the paperwork including pay. Not least he was the custodian of leave and pass forms. Then there was LAC MacDonald who not only looked after the unit health in his capacity as nursing orderly but cut everyone's hair and generally made himself indispensable to the admin side of the unit. LAC Morris as the equipment assistant was involved in all demands for the great variety of supplies that kept the unit running.

The small well run R/T section under Corporal Higginson was a particular asset to the unit providing continuous trouble free radio communication with the aircraft, in addition each member of his section was a competent driver which was of great help during the unit's constant moves. Off duty the section did much of the organization of the unit football team and supplied many of its players, its musical pastimes vocal and instrumental entertained not only themselves but also the rest of the unit on frequent impromptu or formal occasions.

Among our 'characters' the name of Ian Beith comes instantly to everyone's mind who knew the unit. He was one of, if not the youngest and had had a good education which he used for everyone's pleasure or annoyance according to his mood. He dispelled the boredom of many a long night duty by holding forth and leading some erudite discussion or argument. He made the air in the ops room reek with his pipe that was almost invariably filled with Balkan Sobranie tobacco. He was a great writer of poems and together with LAC Blackburn was to encourage the unit towards literary pursuits to be recorded in the unit magazine. His constant battles with Sgt. Poulter were run on fixed rules and each had a mutual respect for the other although no two people were less alike.

December was to be a month devoted to indoor activities as the weather continued to deteriorate and one of our main problems was to fight off the bitter cold of our exposed site. We had kept in reserve some bottles of Calvados that were given to us in Normandy as we considered the spirit to be too strong to be drinkable except in emergency. If one put a match near it there was a little plop and it burnt readily. However, to avert the cold we took to having little nips of this firewater. We also made an assessment of the German trenches and decided that the dangers of dying from cold were greater than from German ground action. We therefore pulled up the fir poles from the sides of the trenches and sawed them up and fed the stoves.

The first major social event of December was on the 7th when the unit held a St Nicholas party for the children of Meeuwen in a local café that was lent to us. Our rotund cook Cpl. Gallop, made a fine St Nicholas and he was backed up by Black Peter whose duties were well carried out by LAC Griffiths of the R/T section. There were no language difficulties and our rations, sweets and chocolate were much appreciated.

The new 83 Group padre paid us a visit and 'our' Light Warning crew 6092 left after being with us for nine months. To add to what little excitement there was in winter in our part of the front a B17 Fortress forced landed right by the site having lost three engines. It was from 35 Bombardment Group at Chelveston and was piloted by a Lt. Whitney. All the crew escaped injury.

On the 13th after a visit from a SHAEF staff officer and football in the afternoon we had a Brains Trust to pass the evening and the more learned and sober members of the unit namely Sgt. Mitchell our senior Ops NCO, and ACs Hynd and Thwaites also of Ops led by our adjutant Flying Officer Taylor gave good entertainment. AC Thwaites in peace-time had the unusual profession of stamp dealer from his offices in Chancery Lane, London.

A week before Christmas the news came through of the break-through by the Germans in the Ardennes and of the retreat by the Americans and of the fierce ground battles that were being fought. The Chief Controller at the GCC got through to me and told me to stand by to move the unit south to cover the German breakthrough. This was all changed half an hour later when I was asked to supply one controller instead, to give surveillance to 83 Group aircraft operating in the American area. The controller would work on the American radar and use their R/T facilities. I welcomed the idea as enemy air activity in our area had been minimal for some time, which was boring and left us with the feeling that we were now making little positive contribution to winning the war. The controller detailed was to report in the first instance to the IXth Tactical Air Force Headquarters in Liege. As it was coming up to Christmas and the New Year I tossed with Hoppy as to which of us should go first and it turned out he would do the first stint.

There was a little extra excitement on Christmas Eve when the Light Warning Unit 6066 recaptured three escaped German POWs. However, Christmas Day was celebrated as well as any unit could celebrate Christmas under the existing conditions. Of course there was no let up from the usual watchkeeping at the radar site and seven SNCOs went on duty at 08.00 in place of the normal crew under the leadership of Flt. Lt. Monty Parker. They were relieved at 11.30 in time to have a quick drink before serving the meal to the airmen in the traditional manner.

After lunch 15119 GCI from their tented site down the road visited us to exchange seasonal greetings and to enjoy the unit Pantomime based loosely on Cinderella, written by LAC Beith with pungent wit directed at most members of the unit. This pantomime was so successful that the players were asked to perform it again at other units. It was in the course of conversation with the officers of 15119 that I learned of the death of 'The Great Brown'. Brown was probably the most famous GCI controller of the war. He controlled the first successful night interception of a German bomber at Sopley GCI on the night of 26th February 1941, and had a long run of successful interceptions with the Beaufighters of 604 squadron stationed at Middle Wallop, for which he was awarded the MBE. There were many stories about Brown and we had had our differences when I was at Hope Cove and he had command of the GCI at Exminster. Brown subsequently took part in the North Africa landings and landed in Normandy on D-Day with 85 Group. At Arnhem he endeavoured to land with two Light Warning units in Hamilcar gliders, but for some reason they could not be set to work and Brown was killed in the fighting. In addition to his MBE, Brown received three 'Mentioned in Despatches'. After Christmas the weather got even colder and we had more snow. On the 28th December the roads were frozen and dangerous when I set off to relieve Flt. Lt. Hopper who was on detachment with the Americans giving surveillance to 83 Group fighter bombers who were reinforcing to counter the German offensive in the Ardennes.

The technical site was very exposed on the old artillery range and going on and off duty from the living accommodation was an endurance test as one fought one's way against the freezing wind. The New Year got off to a good start with the commencement of UK leave, the first lucky members of the unit setting off on January 3rd.

I returned from my detachment with USAF 9th TAC Air Force on the 18th January and went on leave ten days later. The Army had been fighting fierce battles for the Rhineland and was making steady progress. The big news was that the GCC had acquired a radar of its own and after I had only been back from leave a week I was asked to go up and give some instruction on it to the GCC personnel. The GCC was sited in the small village of Erp a few miles east of Eindhoven and on my arrival I was billeted in one of the houses immediately opposite the Catholic church. I used to watch the people each day going into the church before they went to work. Most of them had bicycles which to my astonishment they took with them into the church porch.

I was a little surprised to find that the radar was very similar to the Mobile Early Warning radar (MEW) of the Americans in that it had range rings and azimuth markings as the trace rotated and the off-centring facilities. The consoles were I thought inferior to those of the MEW but for all that it was an excellent radar equipment. It was no surprise to me that there was very little interest shown in the radar by the officer controllers other than the fact that a general air situation could be put on a map in the form of arrows and display plaques without the aid of the FDPs. The officer controllers were happy that the sergeant deputy controllers who normally carried out a listening watch on the operational R/T frequencies should absorb any know-how that was thought necessary.

Sharing the difficulties of trying to persuade the GCC officers of the value of radar in Tactical Air Operations was a Flight Lieutenant from 15053. We were both aware of the impossibility of our task. The deputy controllers were willing to learn but were aware that such learning would be given no official backing. When an aircraft in trouble called with a request for help the only advice he could be given by Kenway was his heading to the GCC obtained from the direction finding equipment operating on the pilot's R/T transmission. When he called for a distance without having been tracked or given surveillance on the radar such help was not available.

I suggested to the chief controller that surveillance of all sorties should be mandatory and that assistance in navigation to targets would bring excellent results, but he said that the bombline was the Rhine and he could see no advantages in the radar surveillance that I proposed. Nevertheless I covered the sorties as best as I could when on watch and one day I more than proved my point. A formation of fighter bombers went off to attack a target and I watched with interest as it went off course and started to wander. I gave a call on the R/T only to receive a sharp reply from the formation leader, "Leave me alone Kenway I am busy map-reading." I gave him another ten minutes, plotting him steadily on the radar as he wandered all over the place obviously lost. I gave another call "Can I help?" and received the reply, "I am having difficulty in locating the target," which was not surprising as he was some way off it. Having asked on which side was his best visibility I directed the formation towards the target pin-point calling out the ranges on the way and the formation leader found the target on his first run-in. Later I phoned him and asked why he had spoken as he did. He said that he was unaware that we were able from the ground to guide him on to his target!

Off duty I was able to enjoy some of the more social life led by the GCC. It was a hard drinking mess, at the small units we had no opportunities of such a life as those at the GCC led. One evening there was an ENSA show and the cast was invited to the Officers' Mess afterwards. For some reason there was a bit argument between two of the GCC officers and I helped to drag them apart as they started to fight. With hindsight I wonder whether I did the right thing as one of the officers was cashiered some months later.

The GCC was always sited near to airfields on which the fighter bombers were based. As a result I was invited to an enjoyable and noisy party at one of them, but I knew none of the pilots and I would have enjoyed rather more the opportunity of a liaison visit to discuss the help we could give to the pilots to make their task easier and safer.

The best success that the officer from '053 and myself had during our time at the GCC was nothing really to do with 83 Group operations. We discovered that among many sources of information available to the GCC was a signal each night of expected activity by the *Luftwaffe*. This came as a result of a breaking of the code for the signal which was sent out to all German flak units of *Luftwaffe* activity for the night. It prevented their own aircraft being fired on. This daily signal was decoded and sent on to the various headquarters units. Having read of expected *Luftwaffe* activity we both turned up that night in the ops room just to watch what would go on. After an hour or so the duty GCC controller told us he was going to the mess and that we should call him if anything happened. In due course German bombers appeared on the radar as forecast by the flak warning signal. GCC had a telephone line to 85 Group responsible for the night defence and with little expectation we gave a call to the controller there and asked if they could spare us a night fighter. To our astonishment we were offered two!

Both of us immediately settled down each in front of a console and proceeded to get organized with radio frequencies and display adjustment and heightfinder information. My aircraft called in and as so often happened it was handed over close overhead and I had great difficulty in locating it. The pilot was obviously nervous at coming under an unknown control and had climbed above the radar coverage at short range. However, when I finally located my aircraft I was able to talk the pilot in steadily to the target as in the old days of night defence in the UK. In fact it was much easier despite the allied night activity going on at the same time. The German bombers were all dropping 'window' or metal strip that was intended to confuse the radar with false echoes. With the new narrow beam width radar all it did however was to identify the track as the allied aircraft were not using 'window' and because of the narrow beam width it only produced a thin tail of response following the aircraft. My pilot acknowledged contact on his target and a little later that he had fired on and destroyed it. I vectored him immediately on to a second aircraft thinking to get as many as he had ammunition for, but to my astonishment he refused it saying he had to return to base. So much for my hopes of having a super night and intercepting several raiders.

The officer from '053 was having the same success as myself when in walked the GCC duty controller. He was furious and I must admit that in the excitement I had forgotten to call him, although his presence would have been of no help. He immediately called out the Group Captain to whom he explained how he as duty controller had done this and that and so on, when in fact he had not been there at all during the interceptions. The two aircraft claimed as destroyed by the pilots under our control was more than the rest of the 85 Group units' total for that night and it was no surprise therefore that no more night fighters were forthcoming from them on subsequent nights.

15054's wish to get on with the war seemed likely to be granted a bit earlier in the year than we might have hoped for. Mac from Group suggested that we should look for a forward site on the line of the projected advance into Germany. He and I and Bill Jones went off into the Rhineland where there had been so much heavy fighting. It was the 6th March and we were a bit unsure of the military situation in the area immediately opposite Wesel and I know it was a bit scary as we went through a track in some wooded country to find an excellent site on what had been an emergency airfield near the village of Bonninghardt about five miles from Wesel across the river. It looked a bit exposed but probably the Germans had more to worry about than a small radar site.

There were no troops about but the area could only have been fought over a short time previously as the houses in the completely deserted village near by were surrounded by clean white sheets and other bedding. When fighting troops went through a village those immediately behind did a quick search of cupboards and drawers for money and valuables. Follow up troops threw out the bedding to make sleeping space sometimes using some of the furniture as fuel. We were shocked to find that the Belgians who had passed through had expressed their distaste for the Germans by leaving excreta on the floor, in the beds and up the walls. There were large stocks of bottled preserves in the cellars but we did not touch them having been warned against booby traps and poisoned food. In one of the houses was an electric washing machine something that we had not seen before. It was later that we were to make good use of it running it from our own electrical supply.

I was still at the GCC when the unit moved some days later, the new site having been declared safe for occupation. Winter had meant an end to 054's well practised mobility and the move on the 11th of March was made in three echelons. The Army moved a battery of medium artillery guns on to the site also and the guns surrounded the radar making things very noisy. There were visits from various staff officers who had not been seen by the unit before, all apparently anxious to claim that they had been in Germany. The Army kept up the artillery barrage through the nights and by the 22nd the roads were full of amphibious vehicles, pontoons and bridging materials indicating that the crossing of the Rhine was not far away.

With all the excitement on 054's site building up I was more anxious than ever to leave the GCC and get back to the unit. Following a night of heavy barrage from the guns, a heavy attack by RAF bombers on Wesel that made the whole earth rumble, in fine weather huge formations of Dakota aircraft passed overhead '054 at low level on the 23rd March to drop gliders and troops. The crossing of the Rhine was under way. To add to the general excitement a Dakota that had been hit, forced landed successfully by the site.

112

Following the successful crossing of the Rhine by the Army I was at last released from the GCC and went back to '054 ready for the next forward rush. The first thing to do was to get the unit a bit more mobile. Everyone seemed to have acquired a lot more personal possessions and these were sorted out and many of them sent home. The weather was excellent and the washing machine we had acquired was doing fine service. We had recovered and washed a lot of the bedsheets that had been abandoned in the village near by and the unit must have been the best laundered in 2nd TAF. So popular was the washing machine that we had to arrange a formal timetable for its use by sections.

A week went by and there was no news of a move. Because we had been the first to move into Germany it looked as though we would have to wait our turn for the next leap ahead. We waited impatiently.

We normally had no contact with the Americans although we were often very close to them, but we saw the regular intelligence reports and noted the daily claims by IXth TAC pilots of enemy war *matériel* attacked, damaged and destroyed. Sometimes they claimed ten times the number of German vehicles, tanks, rolling stock and so on than the 83 Group aircraft. We laughed at the figures attributing them to the usual American habit of exaggeration. I thought that with my years of experience of controlling fighter aircraft on the radar I would be able to give the Americans some tips. How wrong I was!

After Christmas there was a lot of snow and ice about as I drove the forty odd miles down to Liege and I noted the strange defensive posture of the American troops. At each crossroad and bridge there was a tank or two and a small number of troops. Every passing vehicle or pedestrian was stopped and questioned. I was asked to show my ID or identity card, something that had not happened to me since I had landed in Normandy. Not content with this I was then asked to show my vehicle travel authorization and repeat my vehicle number. After being stopped a few times I found it easier to give more information than I was asked for in case I was posed with some question like "Who won the world series?" the answer to which was needed to show I was friendly.

I had one nasty moment on my journey when I passed through a small town crowded with civilians and American traffic. As I was about to descend a steep but narrow street I saw a line of Sherman tanks coming up the hill in the opposite direction. I was travelling very slowly in the jeep but I felt it start to slide slowly on the ice toward a tank on the left just as it was about to pass me. I watched in horror feeling certain I would be crushed but we slid by with barely an inch to spare.

USAF IXth TAC Headquarters was sited in one of the large buildings in Liege itself. My Group Captain from the GCC was there with a few key staff officers such as the chief signals officer and the GCC Army Air Liaison officer to co-ordinate the air reinforcement by 83 Group. The headquarters was very much like the GCC itself at that time in that it had the general air situation plotted on a large map and there was a planning staff to do the tasking of the squadrons. I was directed to the radar or MEW site (Mobile Early Warning) which was a few miles north of the town. I was greeted there by an American officer who invited me along to the 'Chow Line' for lunch saying that Hoppy was busy controlling aircraft but would be along in a while. We went into a large marquee where American airmen were lined up with mess tins in their hands. On the left was a long wooden table to which I was invited. I sat down among a number of American officers and watched as large dishes loaded with chicken pieces and cooked vegetables were passed down. Chicken at that time was unknown as a British Army meal and I was very surprised when a major sitting opposite said in a loud voice, "What, chicken again? I'm sick of chicken." I selected a prime leg for myself only to have my neighbour say, "What's wrong? Don't you like chicken?" Noting that everyone else was taking three or more pieces I helped myself to more. Life with USAF was to be full of surprises.

After the main course came the sweet, large quantities of tinned fruit salad which one ate off the same plate as the chicken course. The airmen queuing with their mess tins improved on this by heaping chicken and fruit salad together in the same tin. The washing-up facilities were the best I have ever seen. Three metal dustbins were kept boiling by means of petrol heaters and the men's mess tins, mugs and irons (knife, fork and spoon) slid on to metal hooks enabling them to be dipped in the water for first wash, second wash and rinse. Because the water was boiling the utensils dried at once despite the freezing cold weather.

After lunch I was taken into the Operations Block and introduced to the senior controller who made me most welcome and proceeded to show me around. My greatest interest was of course the control consoles and the radar display. I sat at the first console and noted with some surprise that instead of the marked grid or map covering the display tube that we used, the unit worked on fine range rings and azimuth marker strobes that came up as the trace rotated. The radar beam width was only one degree wide which made the radar picture very clear with good discrimination between responses. The most interesting advantage of the equipment was the ability to move the rotation centre of the trace in any direction. This meant that any area of special interest could be moved so that it was in the centre of the display and the velocity knob enabled one to enlarge the map-scale at will. On the console were the usual facilities for R/T ground to air to talk to the aircraft, a telephone to the heightfinder and another to the other control consoles.

The main operations room was fairly dark to allow the radar responses to show up well. Each of half a dozen control consoles facing a large
vertical perspex general situation map was manned by a junior officer
controller with fighter aircraft under his control. Airmen behind the
screen plotted aircraft tracks with chinagraph pencils which because of
edge lighting on the perspex showed up clearly. I was told that it was
mandatory for all fighter bomber missions to be given surveillance by one
of the radar controllers. Reporting of the air situation was carried out in
two adjacent vehicles each with a number of displays manned by airmen
plotters who told to the main display screen. The air picture when the
tracks had been marked friendly or hostile was told to TAC Headquarters.

Next to the operations room was the planning room where a large
scale map of the area covered a complete wall. On it were marked range
circles and azimuth from the radar site, airfields and the up-to-date
bombline. The bombline was a line agreed by the Army as a demarkation
between where the ground attack aircraft could attack targets and the
other side where no attacks were permitted. It took into account an area
in front of the allied troops to allow for advances during the day plus a
safety margin.

I was allocated sleeping quarters in the Hotel Moderne in the centre
of Liege where most of the IXth TAC officers lodged including the
general. It was my first billet during the campaign and a great treat to be
in a hotel even if the bedroom door did not close properly due to damage
from the V-1 buzz bombs that landed regularly in the town. I had retired
to bed on my first night there after a tiring day only to be wakened at
intervals either by explosions from falling buzz bombs or female squeals
from the room next door or the noise of women running up and down
the corridor. As I went down to breakfast I was embarrassed to find a
woman descending the stairs in front of me and another just behind. The
food was splendid but the neat unsweetened grapefruit juice, strong
coffee, fried eggs and bacon, pancakes and syrup, together with people
smoking at the table were almost too much for my stomach and it was
the only time in my life that I suffered regularly from a feeling of morning
sickness.

Driving out of town in the morning to the radar site I was often
stopped on the road in the town by American Army sentries. They asked
me for my vehicle work ticket and the usual questions, but after the first
day or so I countered this by slowing the vehicle down long before I
reached the sentries and leaning out and yelling, "My jeep number is

116

one, two, three, four, five and I do not know who won the world series but Crosby's name is Bing." Before I could finally come to a halt I was usually waved on with an "OK Bud" from the sentry.

On the radar site I settled down to giving the 83 Group fighter bombers surveillance whilst they were in the area, identifying the tracks to the Americans to avoid any chance of conflict and passing warnings to my aircraft of any others in their vicinity. During a break I was interested in a discussion between two of the American officers concerning the appearance of an American serviceman that they had seen close by on their way to work. Apparently the man was wearing some item of uniform that was not standard. Since Americans to me never seemed to wear anything standard I was surprised that they noticed. However a bit later on there was a report that the man had been picked up 'in the chow lines' and was in fact one of the Germans infiltrated into the area in American uniform.

I was invited to a New Year's Eve party which turned out to be very enjoyable as a good number of American nurses had been invited to it. I was getting along well with a lovely nursing officer from Alabama until we had language troubles causing a misunderstanding from which a budding friendship did not recover. I had used a common enough RAF expression that was not acceptable to her.

Working on the radar next day there was a sudden call from one of the American controllers that his aircraft had reported that they had sighted German fighter aircraft over their base and were in combat. There was an initial feeling of disbelief as there was nothing to be seen on the radar but this only meant that the raiders must have been very low. Every controller put out a warning to aircraft under his control and there were soon reports coming in of combats with enemy aircraft over other bases. Daylight attacks by German aircraft on airfields was unknown but this was the great New Year's Day attack on allied airfields under the code name HERMANN.

Apart from the time when I had been entertained by Belgian families during our briefest of stops in Brussels, my social contacts since I had been with 15054 had been minimal. The riotous way of living by the Americans in Liege in the middle of a war was a real eye-opener to me. On the first floor of the Hotel Moderne which was the IXth TAC Mess was a large lounge with a bar in one corner that dispensed drinks and cigarettes and other small PX items such as soap and toothpaste. However these items were only available to USAF personnel and it took a good deal of persuasion before we few British were allowed the same

117

facilities. We were then allowed to buy a book of tickets for drinks, all of which were at the same nominal price the equivalent of sixpence or so at that time. Cigarettes and tobacco were also much cheaper than our NAAFI equivalent. Our most favoured drink was Benedictine and brandy mixed.

Just up the road from the hotel was a large cinema and below it a dance hall called 'The Garden of Eden'. It was more popularly known as 'The Evil Gardens'. Every night it was packed almost entirely by American servicemen and civilian women. Among the many interesting people I met there was a young Polish woman and her Dutch girl-friend. They showed me with pride a blood-stained cigarette package that they had taken from a dying German soldier as he was lying in the street having been shot during the liberation of the city. I was revolted.

At the MEW I was very impressed with the efficient way in which the fighter bombers were handled. Not only was each mission given radar surveillance but it was also given navigational assistance and up-to-date information, and direction on to ground targets as they were reported. When a reconnaissance aircraft came up with a report of a train, convoy of vehicles or a concentration of tanks the controllers were allowed to offer the target to the aircraft under their control passing all information on the target and then giving navigational direction to a visual sighting of it. It was a fairly common occurrence to hear a call, "Say, has anyone got any more bombs?" from one controller to the operations room in general and there would be a small discussion of where the target was and what it consisted of. This usually resulted in further fighter bombers being directed over the target within a few minutes. This was the method of working which was envisaged by us RAF controllers when the original 'Fordirect' trials were carried out in the UK.

I enquired from the Chief Controller how it was that the fighter bombers had accepted control from the MEW so readily and that it was mandatory for all sorties to be given radar surveillance. He told me that when they were in Normandy they had noticed a line of slow moving echoes close to the station and had sent an aircraft along to investigate. The pilot had reported a line of German tanks in that position and after that the MEW controllers could do no wrong. It would be uncharitable to suggest that the responses were probably spurious as everyone needs a bit of luck to be successful.

Back at the hotel sitting in the lounge one night there was the usual sound of buzz bombs coming over. Two came over about every twenty minutes but there was no certainty that they would fall in the town. One might fall, both might fall, or else they continued on to fall it was said, in Antwerp. On this occasion one engine cut near by and the bomb started to fall, most of us went flat on the floor with no sense of shame. There was a noise of broken glass falling behind the heavy curtains but nothing else.

The big event of the evening however was the sight of a USAF birdie colonel sitting with and jealously guarding two very pretty young girls. Various American officers approached the table obviously with the thought of joining them but each was rebuffed. I mentioned jokingly to the other RAF officers at the table that I felt sure I knew the girls and this was followed by a challenge that I could not get into conversation with them. I bided my time until the colonel was forced to get up and leave the table to get some drinks. I went over and introduced myself in French to the girls and learned in the short time before the colonel returned that they were students from northern Belgium and that they were living in the hotel and gave me a room number. When the colonel returned I excused myself and went back to my table. Subsequently I rang one of the girls and we had a pleasant evening together going to a French speaking cinema in the town.

Some days later I was asleep in my room one night when the telephone rang. It was Colin Grey the British Army liaison officer whose room was immediately above mine. He said he had just had a telephone call from the girl which had been put through to him by the operator by error. He said she had asked if I would go up to her room right away and he gave me the number. I thanked him and leapt out of bed very happy to have such an invitation. As I was dressing I had a sudden doubt, such a thing had never happened to me before, could it really be true? I rang the girl's room and said that Major Colin Grey had told me about the telephone call and so on only to be told that she had never heard of a Colin Grey and had certainly not phoned him. I immediately rang Colin and told him what a dirty trick I thought he had played on me but he maintained that the girl had phoned and took a very high handed attitude saying he had no wish to be associated in any way with my philanderings. The telephone rang again and it was from the lady who said she had phoned Colin Grey who denied having received any telephone call from her and expressed absolute ignorance as to who she was. I heard sounds of laughter from the room above and realized that the joke was on me.

Calling in at the headquarters on my way to the MEW the next morning I was taken aside by my Group Captain who told me that he had heard that Colonel X was looking for me and as the colonel was a good shot I would be well advised to keep out of his way. I learned later that the Group Captain and the Chief Signals Officer had been having a quiet chat in Colin's room that evening when the telephone rang. It was the young lady in question and swiftly catching on Colin acknowledged that he was me and carried on a long and very friendly conversation with her in French. The rest of the leg-pull followed with his call to me and all of them were party to the affair. I learned also that the girls were actually living with two colonels neither of whom could speak French, which was probably just as well as the girl was in bed with the colonel throughout the whole affair. Both colonels moved out of the hotel with the girls the next day.

Each day at the MEW I became more impressed with the working of the IXth TAC. In 83 Group of which 15054 was a part there were some twenty-one squadrons of fighters, fighter bombers and reconnaissance aircraft on seven mobile airfields. The activities of the squadrons were controlled by a planning staff at the GCC, who provided the daily tasking and times and routes for armed sweeps and recces and also for strikes on specific targets. When a recce aircraft came up with a radio report on a ground target this was immediately passed to the planners for action. They allocated the target to a squadron and detailed the armament and the message was passed to the airfield. The squadron aircraft were armed and the pilots assembled for briefing before take off. Since this meant about two hours before the aircraft arrived over the target it had in many instances disappeared.

I was therefore more anxious than ever to provide some form of ground control rather than surveillance for the 83 Group aircraft as I was convinced it was immeasurably superior. My opportunity came at last when I was allotted eight aircraft of No. 350 Squadron who were to carry out an armed recce in the area. The flying conditions in the Ardennes at the time were very difficult with poor visibility and snow covering the hills and woods making map reading extremely difficult. I had a very recent report of a concentration of vehicles in an orchard, vehicles moving on a road and also a column of marching men. The targets were all within a few miles of each other and very near the bombline. I was astonished and delighted when I was given permission to offer the target to 350 and to give them navigational assistance. I quickly prepared the radar setting the target area in the centre of the display and enlarging the scale. I looked up the large scale map to check ground reference points and marked the bombline on the radar display. To my delight the formation leader, Terry Spencer accepted my offer of the targets and I talked him into the first calling off the clock code and ranges. He picked the target up on his first run in and went down to attack. He then called asking for a check on his position and I said he was only a mile from his first position attack to which he replied "Roger, just checking." I told him of the vehicle convoy on the road to the east and the marching men beyond that. Within a few minutes of arriving in the area the formation was on its way back to base. The squadron achieved a record score of vehicles destroyed that day.

I hoped that this effort would lead to the adoption of some ground radar control of strike aircraft. The advantages were so obvious, aircraft could be brought on to a target within minutes of its being reported, they could be relieved of the work of navigation to the target and work with safety close to the bombline. More important the time of strike aircraft over enemy territory and hence the pilot and aircraft loss rate could be reduced. It was not to be, the squadron commander of 350 Squadron was shot down the next day and so was not available to give me his support. I was not given another chance to control strike aircraft on to a ground target whilst at the MEW.

One day I was surprised to see an RAF pilot at the MEW. I introduced myself and he told me that he had just been shot down by the Americans who had brought him to the MEW. It seems that he was flying low in and out of low cloud in the bad weather and had flown straight over the anti-aircraft battery. The gunners had picked him up and had been most apologetic but he was far from amused. He told me that he had heard of a case where three Tempests out of four had been shot down in the same manner.

The German Army was on the retreat from the Bulge. Taking a breather one day outside the ops room between sorties I was surprised to see General Montgomery stop his car on the high road and relieve himself against a tree. I suppose it was just the cold weather but it made him seem vulnerable to it just like the rest of us. When the need for support by the RAF fighter bombers was over I was ordered back to Meeuwen. I had learned a lot whilst I was with USAF and had a great deal of respect for the way IXth TAC handled their fighter bombers and more understanding of their high claims of enemy vehicles destroyed. I thought they made excellent use of their radar.

Driving back to 15054 I was stopped by a large coloured soldier guarding a bridge over a canal and had to go through the usual list of questions. He let me through but I was surprised to be stopped by another sentry at the far end of the bridge. I explained that I had just been cleared by the other sentry to which he replied, "Not by me you ain't," and questioned me again.

We waited impatiently at the site at Bonninghardt opposite Wesel for orders to move forward to take our usual position as the forward unit of 2nd TAF but they did not come. 15053 had been given the privilege this time and we were later to be regaled with the story of how they had set up their radar in the Rheine area with a Scottish infantry regiment digging in for the night behind them.

We continued to enjoy the good weather and relaxed atmosphere at Bonninghardt until at last on the 10th April we were told to pack and prepare for a rendezvous with the GCC and its new Type 70,000 radar in the Osnabruck area. We packed our radar and waited our movement order for the Rhine crossing. On the 12th we struck the tents, packed everything that we could and slept under the vehicles. After a breakfast at 05.00 the cook's utensils were packed away and we were off. We followed a route marked with large signs directing us to the bridge we were to use.

The crossing of the long temporary pontoon bridge over the Rhine was exciting as was the sight of the wrecked gliders at the side of the road. They had been dropped filled with troops as part of the river crossing attack. We made steady progress on our long move and had made a temporary halt in the town of Osnabruck when to my astonishment a German woman came up to my vehicle and told me that our tall vehicles would not pass under the railway bridge on the road ahead and that we would have to make a detour on a route which she explained to us! Arriving at our given pin-point we found that yet again it was wrong and we spent some time finding the GCC and we pitched our tents some ten miles east of the town. We found it incredible that GCC which used map references every day for plotting purposes and squadron tasking seemed unable to give us any pin-point which was correct.

The following day (14th) Mac, Bill and myself went off looking for a suitable site in the Celle area as instructed. The military situation was now becoming most confused and no one had any idea if, or where, there would be resistance by German troops. We drove on roads that went through a lot of forest and during a brief halt found hidden off the main road a large convoy of new German military vehicles all of which had had their engines smashed with a hammer. I was most disappointed as many of them would have made a welcome addition to our vehicle strength. The following day the padre came to our site and we had an open air service. We also received orders to move off the next day to Eschede north-east of Hanover and await further instructions.

It was the 16th April and not having to pack any of the technical gear we had breakfasted and packed our domestic gear and were on the road by 07.45 for yet another long convoy drive. On the way the Type 13 aerial vehicle had a puncture and we were in the middle of changing a wheel when a civilian came along and insisted on helping saying that he had been a motor mechanic. It appeared that he was one of the foreign workers that had been moved to Germany for war work. Whilst he was changing the wheel I saw a party of about fifty men coming down the road. They tried to ease past me but I stood in the way and one of their number eventually got pushed to the front to act as spokesman. He looked a bit sheepish and produced a paper saying to me, "*Entlassen*" (demobbed). I read the paper which said in English, 'These men are Volksturmer troops that were called up but did not fight. They are to be allowed to travel back to their homes but are not to be given any assistance or transport.' The paper had a British military unit stamp on it. I enquired from the men their home town and they told me somewhere in south-west Germany. I thought they had a long walk ahead of them but they seemed very happy with their lot. They went off to inflict themselves on the next farm for the night.

At the new site once again we did not set up the radar but awaited further orders. The following day the adjutant went off to collect rations and the rest of the unit carried out routine work on vehicles. An advanced party of 2798 RAF Regiment arrived for our protection to be followed the next day by the rest of the Flight. Meanwhile we had found a deserted SS barracks not far away and had spent a great deal of the day acquiring vehicles and equipment that we thought might come in useful. The best items were two staff cars which would be rather nicer than my jeep to travel in and a fully equipped trailer workshop and masses of tools which would be invaluable to us.

Hoppy was away at an 85 Group unit to arrange (at last) for us to do some night interceptions as we were so far forward and one assumes, the 85 Group units were getting left behind. We received orders at midday from GCC to find a site near by and be operational by nightfall as Hoppy and an 85 Group controller would be arriving with us for night interceptions. It was not until the next day however that Hoppy and a Flying Officer Shaw arrived, they unbelievably having been given yet another wrong pin-point by GCC! They brought with them a AI beacon that would enable the fighters to locate us and therefore be able to give their range and bearing from us.

The new site was at Beedenbostel but the site was very damp after the recent bad weather. Two FW 190 German fighters flew over at 07.20 on our first morning and then circled low enough for the pilots to be seen clearly. We had acquired a machine-gun for air defence but did not fire it at them as the aircraft behaviour did not seem hostile and we wondered if they would land at one of the nearby airfields and surrender. GCC seemed to have lost interest in receiving an air picture and we were not required to man during the day and although we switched on the AI beacon and manned the R/T frequencies for three nights we had no call from any night fighters.

We were only a few miles from the concentration camp at Bergen Belsen and there were a number of ex-inmates moving around on the roads dressed in the distinctive striped camp suits. The camp however, still contained a large number of men, women and children. On the 23rd following an appeal from the Red Cross we had managed to fill a three-tonner with clothing, blankets and food plus a personal collection of cigarettes, chocolates and sweets and these were taken along by two of the unit who made the necessary contacts and saw a lot of the camp and met some of the inmates. They were shocked beyond describing, as most of us were by the things they saw.

On the 25th April there was a bit of excitement when we, assisted by our RAF Regiment following up local information brought in the local Gestapo chief and took him into Celle where we handed him over to the Army Military Police who were delighted. It appeared that he was at the head of their wanted list although his name meant nothing to me. The adjutant arriving back from an admin run to the GCC brought back orders for us to move to the Luneburg area and Bill Jones and myself set off the next day on a siting expedition leaving the rest of the unit to pack the technical gear as we were not doing any operational plotting. We travelled through some pleasant country and here and there passed small parties of German soldiers up to thirty or more, marching behind a leader who carried some form of white material on a pole. We ignored them as we had not troubled to take any prisoners since the beginning of September last when we had crossed the Seine.

124

We found a most superior open grassland site at a village called Horndorf not far from the town of Lauenburg north-east of Luneburg. Returning to the old site we moved off early the next day and had arrived at the new site at Horndorf by midday and set up the gear. We were once again plotting the air situation to the GCC. We had with us 6092 Light Warning which was set up near by and the RAF Regiment Flight. It was the Regiment that was to cause me some embarrassment. We had been buying eggs from the local farmers using our occupation money when the Regiment told me they had acquired a pig and offered some fresh pork for the benefit of the officers. I enquired as to how they had obtained the pig and was told that one of the local farmers had insisted that some of the Regiment lads should accept the pig as a present as a token of his goodwill. As the pig was dead there was little that I could say. The fresh meat was delicious and a welcome change from the Compo rations but I forbade the men to acquire any more meat knowing what a thin line there was between buying, commandeering and looting.

Driving into the town of Luneburg to locate Army supply centres I was amazed to see a long line of German soldiers four deep, queuing to enter a POW camp. The queue seemed to extend half-way round the town. By now the Army had crossed the Elbe at Lauenburg near by and had allocated times at which our troops could use it one way and German troops surrendering could use it in the other direction, the war was obviously fast coming to an end. A short way to the east of the site there was a road running to the south that was filled with a slow moving column of German military vehicles heading towards a surrender assembly point. There were wheeled vehicles and half-tracks, armoured vehicles and guns and ammunition carriers.

Most of the troops were quiet and sad looking but some had been drinking heavily and were singing. A lucky few had women with them. Standing at the side of the road waving the vehicles on I noticed a German soldier changing into civilian clothing behind some bushes. I gently waved my revolver to point in the direction of the road and yelled, "*Heraus*" which I thought was a good German expression for that sort of situation. The result was most effective as the half-dressed soldier leapt out from the bushes on to the road and into the next vehicle in the slow moving line. I noticed that none of the soldiers wore a wrist watch, it being customary at that time for any surrendering soldier to be forced to hand over his watch to his captor or any other soldier that spotted it.

There was little enemy air activity to be seen on the radar, just the odd track at some range. On the 30th we controlled a continuous fighter patrol over the Elbe bridge-head but there was no enemy opposition. On the 3rd an Auster landed by the site short of fuel. We produced some ordinary MT petrol and he put it in his tank and took off again safely. The weather turned most miserable with a little snow that changed to rain and it was cold.

It was about this time that I acquired a very fine sheepskin flying jacket that I was to wear for some years. It was being worn by a German airman who I suspect had acquired it in turn from some allied airman that had been shot down. The German was reluctant to part with it but I insisted and in a fit of compassion gave him a new *Luftwaffe* overcoat from a stock we had in case he needed it in the POW camp. An Army despatch rider arrived on the site and was brought to me. He said he had lost a German division and had I seen one around? I wondered for a moment if he was mentally deranged but he explained that he had been made responsible for conducting a German division that had surrendered but he could not find it!

I was intrigued by the story and went off on my own in the jeep to look around the local villages although it was getting rather late in the day. I came across a small village that, to my great surprise had apparently been taken over completely by German troops. There were ambulances and other military vehicles parked all around and there were military signs everywhere indicating the location of various sub units and sections. Uniformed German officers and men were busily hurrying in and out of the houses. I gathered from the general military markings that I was probably in the middle of a German SS Division Field Hospital. Everyone was far too busy to take any notice of me but as it was getting dark I thought it would be most indiscreet of me to hang about and I returned to our site.

On the 4th of May we had a message just before lunch that Mac was arriving from Group and that we would be off on a siting trip. Immediately after lunch Mac and Bill and I set off. Crossing the bridge over the Elbe after the usual traffic hold up we headed north. Later we found ourselves on the autobahn leading towards Bad Oldesloe. It was a most odd feeling as the autobahn was completely deserted and as we drove along we could see no troops at all in the countryside either. We had no idea how far our own troops had advanced or if we were at risk from enemy action. We made our way generally northwards and at one point found ourselves coming up to a tee junction where to our consternation a large German staff car was halted and some obviously very senior German officers were consulting a map. We stopped and quickly reversed until we were out of

126

sight and able to turn.

Eventually we found ourselves about six miles south of Neumunster where we were stopped by a small detachment of the Inns of Court Recce Regiment who had put up a road block. They informed us that there was a 'Standstill' order on and that there were to be no troop movements past them. The unit was occupying itself smashing up a huge pile of small arms that they had collected from German soldiers, houses and farms round about. The pile included some very fine shotguns and hunting rifles that had been taken in house searches and which we admired. The Army told us as a matter of interest that there were some 30,000 SS troops in the town of Neumunster just a few miles away. A few unarmed Germans in uniform approached the road block waving papers and calling "Entlassen" (demobbed) but the soldiers waved them away telling them to come back with their general.

There was nothing more to be done than to return to the site at Horndorf. Setting off back south we ran into the outskirts of Hamburg. The damage inflicted by air raids on the city was terrible. As far as one could see there were only the towering ruins of bombed buildings. The main road was clear but all the side roads were blocked with rubble. It was beginning to get dusk and twice I had completed a circuit and arrived back at the same point. I got out of the vehicle hoping to see an Army unit or someone who could direct me. There had been no announcement that the city had been taken and we were very uncertain of what to expect.

Two German policemen appeared suddenly from around a building and seeing me in my peaked cap instinctively threw up their hands in a Heil Hitler salute. I asked the policeman the way but neither of them appeared to understand English. By now it was beginning to get dark. I was sick at the sight of so much destruction and very worried that I might not be able to find my way out of the city before dark. Driving along I suddenly noticed a block of flats that appeared occupied and little damaged. I got out and rang the bell on one of the flats. To my surprise and relief the door opened and I was faced with a young and attractive woman to whom I explained in English that I was unable to find the road to Lauenburg. I was even more surprised when the woman answered in excellent English and gave me clear directions. We had no trouble from then on in finding our way back to site in the dark. I never saw the woman again.

Later that evening listening to the BBC news we received the news flash of the German surrender. The war in Europe was over at last.

Early next day, following the announcement of the surrender I went with Bill Jones back up towards Neumunster, this time without the uncertainties of the day before and the fear of enemy action. I had been thinking of the excellent shotguns and hunting rifles that the army had been smashing up and thought that I could offer a good home to one of them. When we got back to the village where we had been stopped by the Inns of Court recce car squadron it was to find I was too late. The army had destroyed everything that they had collected. Bill and I went on into Neumunster but the army had already been in there too and made certain arrangements making it impossible for us to proceed any further with the idea of finding a site further north.

When we returned to the Horndorf site there was a message from Wing Commander Loud at the GCC that we were to move to Travemünde and take over the *Luftwaffe* base there. We looked for its location on the map and it seemed a good place to go. It was a thrilling thought to be taking over a *Luftwaffe* base especially one right on the Baltic coast. Dismantling of the aerials and packing of the unit was already underway. We were on the road early next morning, the adjutant and I going on ahead to check that the route was OK and to find what facilities and accommodation there were, on the airfield. We were in for a number of surprises most of which were very pleasant. The first surprise was to find that our approach to the *Luftwaffe* base had to be via a vehicle ferry across from the town of Travemünde on to the Priwall where the base was. The airfield area was in fact almost an island.

As we drove up the road after coming off the ferry the airfield lay to our right beyond some cultivation with a group of hangars at the far end. We found the main entrance on the right, between some large hangars and an administrative block, whilst opposite the main entrance on the left there were other large barrack blocks. Driving in through the gate there were more surprises as in front of us was an enormous concrete hard facing an inland sea, more giant hangars, a large six engined flying boat out of the water apparently undergoing overhaul and across the water on the far shore yet more hangars.

There was to be no hand over of the base to us. The Luftwaffe, about two thousand strong we understood, were confined to their barracks and our instructions were that any contact between us was to be minimal. The remainder of the unit arrived just after lunch together with the RAF Regiment Flight. We parked the vehicles on the hard happy not to have to put up the radar and set about finding our way around. We went into the headquarters building and it seemed appropriate that I should make myself comfortable in the office of the previous CO and take over his large stand of rubber stamps of which that of SEEFLIEGERHORSTKOMMANDANT was the most impressive. The stamps were to be most useful in the coming days to back up orders and demands I made on the Germans.

Together with the RAF Regiment Flight we numbered about a hundred men, but there was room for us all with comfort in the large building. It was to feel strange to live in a brick building after so long in tents and huts. The war with Japan had still to be won so we put out guards not only to protect our own equipment but everything on the base in case it should be needed for the war in the Far East. The sun shone and with the war over the immediate future for us looked very bright.

I made contact with the local Army unit, a company of the Argylle and Sutherland Regiment who had been tasked with the manning of the border with the Russian Zone. This ran only a hundred yards or so from the main gate and the army had erected a barrier across where the land narrowed. The Russian Zone border in fact cut the *Luftwaffe* base in two, since the hangars that we could see across the water were now in Russian territory. The Russians were not yet there, as British paratroopers had reached Wismar to the east and had not yet been withdrawn.

On the Baltic beach side of the barrier were a number of holiday homes housing German civilians. On the other side were a number of huts that were the living quarters of foreign workers who had been employed on the base. It appeared that in addition to the *Luftwaffe* personnel there were another two thousand people on the Priwall.

A German Hauptmann appropriately named Führer reported to me as interpreter and liaison officer. He spoke good English and before the war had been a pilot on the Lufthansa South American routes flying the giant Dornier flying boats. I found him very pleasant and we were to get on well together. He showed me an excellent kitchen and a superb dining room to go with it and found me half a dozen kitchen helpers from the hundreds of foreign workers. They were Russian women of assorted ages and we had no common language, they looked at us as though they were in fear of their lives.

The base was almost intact having only had a few bombs scattered over the hard, although a freighter anchored out in the bay had been attacked by RAF fighter aircraft with rockets, and had been abandoned. The next day we set about making ourselves comfortable. Electricity was restored as was hot water. In addition to the kitchen staff we organized two of the civilian boatmen to man the two flying boat tenders and also to provide any technical help we might need with things such as the 400 ton floating crane.

We were obviously on a combined airfield and flying boat base, plus something to do with FW 190 fighters as there were some partly assembled in one of the hangars. There were also two small submarines out of the water alongside the headquarters building. We discovered that there were in fact three separate establishments forming the base. These were Lufthansa and an Experimental Unit based on the Priwall and the section known as ZA on the far side of the bay. Lufthansa was the originator of the base back in 1938 when it put up the first hangar. Throughout the war it carried out repairs on Junkers 52 and Junkers 90 transport aircraft a number of which were dispersed around the airfield. In the latter stages of the war Lufthansa assembled wings, undercarriages and special equipment for the FW 190 fighters.

The largest work of the base was that of the Experimental Unit which carried out repair work on the giant BV 222 flying boats and also the BV 138s. The ZA was a storage and repair depot for all sorts of seaplanes, and more recently was engaged in the electrical wiring and fitting of instruments to FW 190 fuselages before passing them over to the main section of the base for assembly. The workforce of all the units comprised mixed nationalities but without delving too deeply into things we were satisfied with the following incomplete breakdown. Lufthansa: German numbers unknown, plus 120 Dutch and 80 Russians, Experimental 500 Germans plus 150 Italians and ZA 1,000 mixed German, French and Latvians.

With no watch duties the lads were relaxing and looking around enjoying the sunshine and the feeling that 'it was all over'. Two of them came to me and explained that when exploring further up the coast they had found that the *Luftwaffe* had a number of yachts complete with all sails and rigging which were stored in Neustadt and asked my permission to bring one or two of them to the Base where we could make use of them. It seemed a good idea to me and I agreed on the basis that it seemed reasonable to bring them in for safe custody.

We were somewhat surprised to receive visits from a number of officers from the GCC nominally on duty. We had never had visits from them before and concluded they were there to see what they could acquire. Later three officers of the GCC were to be court-martialled on charges of looting, arson, theft and rape and subsequently cashiered. The news came through that VE Day (Victory in Europe) was to be celebrated on the 8th and we started to make arrangements for a celebration party to be held in the evening. It was a tremendous relief to know that after all the years of stress, fear and deprivation, the war in Europe at least was over. Most of the unit relaxed by playing football, swimming or sleeping.

Our VE Day celebrations were to start with a pyrotechnic display. From the *Luftwaffe* stores and offices we had acquired a large stock of Very lights and pistols, flares and rockets. Everyone was assembling on the hard for the commencement waiting for it to get dark, when there was the sound of an aircraft and we saw a German flying boat circling in the half light. It flew even lower and landed on the water in front of the hard. Our German boatmen had gone off duty some time before so I called to the adjutant and he and I and a couple of the lads ran to the pier and leapt into one of the motor boat tenders. I started it and steered it towards the flying boat which we now recognized as a three engined BV 138. On approaching the flying boat a small hatch in the front end of the aircraft opened up and a crewman held out a towing rope which we took with the idea of towing the aircraft to one of the buoys. However, I had no experience of driving a motor boat let alone towing a flying boat. What subsequently followed was annoying to the flying boat crew, horrifying to me and apparently amusing to many of the watchers. At our first pull nothing seemed to happen for a while and then the flying boat came rushing towards us at an angle and the propellers seemed dangerously near. The flying boat then went off at an angle the other way and there was much shouting and gesticulation from the flying boat crewman. After a few more nasty moments the pilot shut down two engines and finally the third and at last we were near enough to one of the buoys to grab it and make the flying boat fast.

I then managed with some difficulty to get the motor boat alongside the flying boat on the entrance side when the door opened. I urged the crew out into the boat together with the fairly small amount of kit they had brought with them. I asked the pilot where he had come from and he told me Tromso in north Norway. He complained bitterly about the poor way in which his aircraft had been handled on landing. He asked how far the Russians were away and I told him that the border actually ran through the Priwall and he was visibly shaken. I gathered that his family were living not far away, probably in what is now the Russian Zone.

I assumed that the pilot was probably more skilled in handling a motor boat than I was after his criticism of my handling of the mooring, so, I asked him to take over the motor boat and steer us to the pier. It was almost dark by now and the first phase of the VE celebrations were underway. The Very lights were being fired off together with the flares and maroons and they looked very impressive. However, as we got nearer to the pier the Very lights which had been directed out over the water for safety reasons were descending all around us and appeared to be increasing in number. It was getting rather dangerous I thought. The German pilot acted as though he was in mortal danger and I myself felt forced to give a very shrill order for the display to stop. Having landed safely back at the pier the flying boat crew were taken to the German barracks and we went on with the VE celebrations.

The pyrotechnic display was followed by a memorable party in the dining-room. It was the unit's first and last party. The cooks had prepared a huge supper from hoarded goodies and this was served by the officers in Christmas fashion. We had acquired a reasonable amount of wine and beer and this was augmented with the whole of the unit rum ration which we held for emergencies. After the meal and a few words of appreciation from myself for the way everyone had worked together, thanks that we had all got through and a short review of results we had achieved, we moved on to some competitive games which developed into a free for all. All the stresses of the war were worked off that evening in a terrific party in which sadly the large pictures of the German hierarchy which adorned the walls were smashed together with the drums of the band and a few more things beside. This unforgettable party was recorded in the Ballad of '054 written at the time . . . 'Though the war they'd survived . . . .' by Ian Beith which is at the start of this story.

The following morning I consulted with the boatmen as to the best action to be taken about the flying boat which had arrived the previous night. From them I learned that there were in fact two, the other having landed in the sea on the Baltic side which had been recovered by the Germans living in the barrack blocks. I arranged for both aircraft to be towed-in and lifted out of the water. The senior boatman asked me who had secured the flying boat to the buoy the previous evening and I admitted that I had done so. The boatman was apparently rather surprised and embarrassed at hearing this, but explained to me with some care that I should have secured the aircraft to the chain underneath the buoy and not to the rubber ring on top as I had done. I was most impressed later to see the flying boats being lifted out of the water by the 400 ton crane which was now part of our unit.

We had now in just a day or so acquired three sailing boats and were able to form a unit Sailing Club complete with the necessary rules and regulations to ensure the safety of the airmen and boats. The three boats were a Sharpie, an Olympia and a keel boat cruiser which I assume must have been one of the 50 square metre boats that were later to form the basis of the Combined Services 'Windfall' yachts. The boats were to provide a great source of pleasure to the lads as we had some enthusiastic and competent sailors amongst us. AC Asgill was the keen Commodore of the Club ably assisted by AC Wright. One afternoon a gale blew up and I was concerned for the safety of one of the smaller boats which was afloat, and went out in one of the motor boats to look for it. The concern was unnecessary as the airmen had merely gone ashore and waited until the blow had ceased.

Whilst out in the tender I came across an RN officer in a small motor boat who had been tasked with keeping an eye on water-borne traffic. He complained that everyone seemed to have a better boat than he had! At that time sailing meant nothing to me although long after the war I was to get a great deal of pleasure from both dinghy and off-shore sailing. Our 'Commodore' of the Sailing Club persuaded me to go out for a trip in the keel boat and on our return asked me what I thought of it. I regret that at the time I said, 'I cannot think of a more frightening and uncomfortable pastime'.

We were all surprised when we saw a large motorised barge flying the Dutch flag come alongside the pier and tie up. The captain bore a note to me signed by the Town Major of Lübeck who requested an early return of the barge as it was urgently required for the transport of vital supplies. The barge was full of components, wings and so on for Ju 52 aircraft. I called for Hauptmann Führer who arranged for the necessary labour and handling equipment to unload the barge which would be a long process because of the quantity of spares involved.

The extraordinary orders of 'non-fraternization' with the Germans were being rigidly enforced. It was most difficult when children and young women called to the lads, "Tommy, Tommy, what is wrong that you will not speak to us?" It was a ridiculous ruling that was followed a few weeks later by an even more incomprehensible one that German troops were not to salute British officers! The one order convinced the German women and children that we really were the T-Flieger or Terror airmen, and the other confirmed to the German armed forces that we really did not know what we were doing.

My time of trial had arrived. On the barge which was flying the Dutch flag was an attractively shaped, scantily clad, young girl who was disporting herself and soaking up the sun. The whole unit was on edge waiting to see who would get to her first. It was then that Hauptmann Führer gave me the bad news. "That girl is German!" I felt I needed extra guards to hold back the lads and was thankful when the barge was at last unloaded and left.

We had not been on site for many days when we had the first major administrative crisis. Apparently all services, electric, heating and running of the ferry would break down unless more fuel oil was obtained. The German electrical engineer was able to supply details of tankers that were available off Lübeck and Monty Parker was sent off to try and obtain the necessary fuel. Monty found one of the tankers, got in touch with the Navy and came to a sharing arrangement with them that gave us a supply of oil to go on with.

I had made a couple of trips over to the BZ unit in the Russian Zone. On the first I just had a quick look around. There were a great number of wooden crates in the hangars, many of which had been opened by looters, and as they contained aircraft instruments of no real use to the opener the instruments had been dropped on the floor. However, others had come and not believing the evidence of the one instrument dropped on the ground had opened yet another package with the same result. On the second trip I collected a number of aircraft clocks which I issued to the men as a token reward since they were guarding stuff to prevent wholesale looting. I also had a look at about two dozen motor boats which were out of the water. I earmarked a very fine large white one with two huge propellers and on my return told the boatmen that I would like them to get it into the water and bring it over to the Priwall side.

Looking in the FW 190 assembly hangar I noticed that the oleo legs of one that was completely assembled had been hit with a piece of hard metal that would ensure that the leg would collapse when the aircraft landed. It was shortly after this that I heard the sound of an aircraft engine and found one of the aircraft being taxied. I waved it down and found in it a pilot from one of the airfields. He had every intention of taking the aircraft away but I told him that it had been sabotaged. He got out of the

134

aircraft and I had the cuts in the oleo legs filed down by a German fitter so that they were no longer dangerous. Regretfully I thought the RAF pilot was less than gracious when I let him fly the aircraft away.

I decided that a FW 190 aircraft would be a most acceptable present to any of the RAF squadrons so I asked Führer to arrange for the necessary manpower to start up the assembly line again and to paint the finished aircraft with RAF roundels.

On the airfield I discovered a small biplane rather like a Tiger Moth but smaller. I understood it was a Fokke trainer and Führer assured me it was serviceable, so I asked him if he would take me up for a trip. He said that his last flying had been on multi-engined flying boats, but I said I was not worried and on the following day after the aircraft had been serviced we went up for a short flight and had a look around the area.

It was a very odd feeling to be flying over Germany in a small aircraft now that the war was over. It was a glorious sunny day and we just flew round about the base looking at the beaches and being careful to keep inside the British Zone. I had every confidence in Führer's ability to manage such a small aircraft and he told me that he enjoyed the trip very much.

The Group Signal Officer arrived at the unit waving his arms and shouting that our W/T section had been blocking out the Group Guard frequency by continually sending out the unit call sign. We had not unpacked the W/T vehicles since our arrival and my corporal i/c the W/T section backed me on this. Therefore, I assured him, it could not have been our operators. Anyway, I said our W/T sets were not powerful enough to jam the frequency as we normally had great difficulties in making contact. I also told him that his operators would instantly recognize the individual keying of my operators. To this he replied that they had, which puzzled me somewhat, but I stuck to my story. It was not until some months later that I found my W/T section had discovered on the airfield a powerful transmitter which had been used for long range communication with the flying boats. They had switched it on and tuned it to the Group Guard frequency and transmitted the unit's call sign.

The fine weather continued and everyone was having a good time relaxing. There was a lot of lying in the sun, swimming, sailing, going out in the motor boats, playing football and preparing for a sports day. Some had even found opportunities for horse riding. A Canadian photographic unit had been attached to us from the Group reconnaissance wing. They were a welcome addition as they found on the base two photographic laboratories and a unit photographic club was immediately started. I was asked by one of the Canadians if I would like to have my photograph taken. He was a photographer by profession and said he had paid more in income tax before the war than all he was paid by the RCAF. He took my photograph with a plate camera when I was wearing my everyday battledress. By shading the plate my shirt collar was made even cleaner and it gave me a better shave so that the result was in my opinion a good film star picture of myself.

The Canadian unit had brought with them some revolting photographs that they had taken of the open mass graves at Belsen, which some of '054 had visited but they had not taken photographs as we had no cameras on the unit until just before the end of the war. In the office among the many administrative problems referred to me was a visit from a German woman doctor who appealed to me for the release of tentage to accommodate German refugees from the Russian Zone. With the pictures I had seen of the conditions at Belsen I was not very well disposed towards Germans at that time and I produced the photographs and held forth to the doctor until she burst into tears. There seemed however, to be no point in withholding permission for the tentage and I released it.

Late one evening there was a panic search when one of the Russian helpers in the kitchen was reported missing. She was found at last in our kitchen where she normally worked and was quietly content peeling potatoes! The teams for repatriation of foreign workers were now active and I do not know if there was any connection, but we had to open up the Base mortuary for two dead Russians who had drunk themselves to death on wood alcohol. A day or so later we saw the last of our Russian helpers in the kitchen when they were taken away for repatriation.

Good progress was made on the FW 190 assembly line and I asked Hauptmann Führer if he could arrange to have the first aircraft coming off the line to be test flown. Führer found a Ju 88 pilot in the German barracks who volunteered to fly the FW 190 on its flight tests. The aircraft duly took off and flew around for a while and then returned. Minor adjustments were made to the ailerons and the aircraft was run up and took off again. To my horror as the aircraft took off so the engine coughed and misfired. I had visions of the aircraft crashing and all the row there would be when, to my great relief, the engine seemed to clear itself. The pilot on his return having apparently enjoyed his flight told me the aircraft was acceptable. The next day a pilot from 127 Wing arrived to collect the aircraft from 15054's own production line.

The administrative problems continued to be of interest. There had been a sudden storm and our 400 ton floating crane had broken adrift and had to be moved back into position and secured. A German civilian technician arrived one day and asked for an interview and explained that he had been engaged on technical research on infra-red guidance systems on aircraft launched rockets and wished to offer his services to the Allies. We took him along and handed him over to the army technical force dealing with that sort of thing.

Hoppy and I went out in one of the motor boats to the abandoned freighter in the bay and we saw the enormous damage caused by the sixty pound aircraft launched rockets that the RAF's Typhoon aircraft carried. They tore through the inch thick steel like a fist going through paper and even little fragments of shell went through the metal too.

Among the major activities of the unit at this time was the production of a summary volume of the unit magazine using reproduction facilities found on the Base. LACs Beith and Blackburn were the joint editors and they had done most of the work of production of the 90 page volume. However, they had persuaded eighteen others of us each to produce an article towards it.

There were still many things that we had yet to attempt. In a corner of a hangar we found an autogyro that was probably designed to be towed from a U-boat and we would have liked to have tried it out towed behind the jeep. There were also the miniature six man submarines that we had not yet really inspected.

It was not to be. On the 18th of May the guards brought in an unknown airman who had been found on the camp with a looted radio. He was the first of the advance party of the Air Disarmament Wing recently arrived from the UK, which was to take over the base and arrange for the disposal of the *Luftwaffe* weapons and equipment. The newly arrived officers talked a strange language of nothing but how to acquire a Luger, parachute silk, a Leica camera and a Mercedes car for themselves. The rest of the ADW party arrived but for us of '054 the glories and enjoyment of Travemünde were over. I watched the big white motor boat arrive at the quay knowing that I would never be able to use it. Signals came in posting some airmen away and another ordering us to move up to Leck and take up our role of FDP once again.

15054 FDP had finished the war hard up against the Russian Border. We could look back knowing that we had played our part well and could think of '054 as being the leading and best ground unit of 2nd TAF. We had been at risk and most of us had been frightened, we had been lucky to have survived. With the war in Europe over we had made the most of our short stay at the magnificent base at Travemünde, and left with much regret.

Every member of the unit was now in doubt as to his future. How long would the war with Japan go on? Who would be sent to the Far East? To the UK? There was talk of demobilization but not for the radar trades. We no longer thought in terms of pushing forward but 83 Group planned that we should still be their most forward unit. Leck our new home was in sparsely populated cattle grazing country within a few miles of the German border with Denmark. We all wondered what the future had in store for 15054.

Extract from the 15054 Summary Magazine 1944/45
Travemünde, Germany, May 1945

The 15054 Chorus
by
Ian Beith

Side by side
We'll stand together
Side by side
No matter whether
Radar Op.; Wireless Op., RT or Mechanic,
Clerk GD, Cook, MT, we shall never panic.

Side by side,
Kemp's Circus we are;
Side by side,
Jim Poulter's Army;
Come what may, any day, we can always take it,
Though we bind, you'll always find We can take it.
SIDE BY SIDE

From the unit pantomime . . . . Winter '44 at Meeuwen

APPENDIX 1

Technical Equipment

RADAR Each radar equipment was known and referred to by its Type Number, e.g. the Type 15 aerial or the Type 15 Ops vehicle. By the time the unit embarked for France it had been issued with three separate radars. They were:

Type 15 A 1.5 metre wavelength search radar with an in-built height finding capability and IFF interrogator. The console presentation was a PPI with a separate 'A' scope for the height-finder operator. The aerial rotation was governed by a control box alongside the controller.

The maximum pick-up range on a large aircraft at height was 120 statute miles. Once an incoming aircraft was picked up the coverage was 'solid', i.e. a response was seen on most rotations of the aerial. The main disadvantage was the wide beam width of more than 15 degrees which produced very long responses and which made controlling difficult, as the picture became unclear when there were several aircraft tracks in the area. The IFF interrogator which enabled identifying responses to be received from Allied aircraft showed as a secondary response on that of the original.

Type 11 A 25cm wavelength search radar. It had a parabolic reflector and the aerial was easily put into operation as the ends folded for travelling. The advantages of this radar were that it could be more easily used on an elevated or uneven site. The whole aerial could be tilted to obtain the best coverage. Its beam width was only 7 degrees giving a much smaller echo and therefore less cluttered picture.

The pick-up performance of this radar was slightly better than that of the Type 15 but incoming aircraft 'faded' or disappeared as they passed through the vertical coverage lobe pattern. Whilst the radar had no height finding capability it was possible to estimate heights from the ranges at which the aircraft appeared or faded as they passed through the coverage.

Type 13 A specialist height finding radar which operated on 10cm wavelength. The crescent moon shaped aerial nodded up and down continuously scanning a narrow vertical section of sky. The presentation to the height operator nodded up and down in the same way and an aircraft showed as a short vertical line on horizontal height lines on the display. The direction in which the aerial faced was shown as a line of light on the Type 11 display and the operator could turn the aerial to face in the direction of the aircraft whose height was required.

COMMUNICATIONS The unit required two types of communication, ground to air in order to control or pass information to the aircraft and ground to ground to pass the air picture to the GCC, maintain operations communications with them and to receive administration signals from Group headquarters.

Ground to Air The unit possessed four R/T (radio telephony) channels for direct speech between the controller and the pilots of the fighter aircraft. The VHF frequencies on which we operated were crystal controlled and all communication was dependent on having the correct crystal frequencies and knowing which frequencies to operate on.

The four transmitters were housed in one Austin six wheeled chassis and the receivers in another. The transmitters and receivers were generally kept some distance apart and away from the Type 15 which could be badly affected by harmonics on one or two of the frequencies used. The aerial dipoles were mounted on high masts whose erection is described in the Renscombe Chapter.

Ground to Ground The unit had four W/T (wireless telegraphy) channels housed in vehicles as for the R/T, although the aerials were simple telescopic types fitted to the vehicles. It was intended that when telephone lines were not laid or were broken that we would operate a plotting channel and a Group Guard administrative channel. Since plain language in wartime was forbidden on W/T it meant that tactical operational messages had to be passed from GCC via the aircraft.

In practice it was found that when we were forty miles or so from the GCC W/T communication was very unreliable, reception being dependent on terrain, weather and times of day. For this reason once we left Normandy we often had small ground to ground VHF units attached to us. This made direct speech possible with the GCC and simplified plotting and general liaison for the taking over of aircraft for control.

APPENDIX 2

Personnel

Operators	*RDF Fitters*	*R/T Section*	*W/T Section*
Sgts.	**F/Sgt.**	**Cpls.**	**Cpl.**
Mitchell	White	Higginson	Holloway
Phillips	**Sgt.**	Scales	
Stubbs	Stevens		
Cpls.	**Cpls.**		
Baker	Lithgow		
Bluett	Doxey		
Dring			
Hancock			

Technical ACs

Asgill	Clarke	Frazer	Hunnam
Banham	Cowan	Hardy	Parker
Beith	Derwent	Hynd	Lockhart
Blackburn	Elsdon	Greening	Nettleton
Birkett	Freeman	Jones	Topliss
Watson	Thwaites	Wooley	Sigsworth
Spathekey	Shaw	Taylor	Wright

ACH/GD	*Transport*	*Cooks*	*Cipher*
Sgt.	**Cpl.**	**Cpl.**	**Sgts.**
Poulter	Bennet	Gallop	Davenport
Cpl.	**LACs**	**LAC**	Fozzard
Harrison	Coogan	Saxton	
ACs	Duckworth		
Fordham			
Head			

Clerk Accounts	*Medical Orderly*	*Equipment Assistant*
Cpl.	**LAC**	**LAC**
Lindley	MacDonald	Morris

APPENDIX 3

The Convoy

When the unit was on the move the vehicles usually travelled in a set order. I normally led the convoy in my jeep with the overloaded out-of-gauge vehicles immediately following. This facilitated command and as the heavier vehicles were restricted to a sustained maximum speed of 20 miles an hour they set the convoy speed which varied according to the road surface and traffic and weather conditions.

The MT Section brought up the rear repairing any faulty vehicle or putting it on tow. When, because of low bridges the tall vehicles had to be detached and go off route I normally drove one of them and handed over the main convoy to Flt. Lt. Hopper.

Lead Vehicle	Jeep (self)	
	* Type 13 Aerial (461A)	Austin Six Wheel
	* Type 15 Aerial	do
	* Type 15 Transmitter	Crossley
	Type 15 Receiver/Ops	do
	Type 11 Aerial	Austin Six Wheel
	Type 11 Ops	do
	3 ton Ops Sectn GP	Crossley
	3 ton Tech Sectn GP	do
	Diesel No 1 (456)	Austin Six Wheel
	Diesel No 2	do
	Diesel No 3	do
	Diesel No 4	do
	VHF Receivers (150)	do
	VHF Transmitters (100)	do
	W/T Receivers	do
	W/T Transmitters	do
	** Cipher	Bedford 15 cwt
	Cooks vehicle	Ford 30 cwt
	Water Bowser (1312)	Bedford 15 cwt
	3 ton GP No 3 (1300)	Crossley
	3 ton GP No 4	do
	3 ton GP No 5	Bedford
	3 ton No 6 (MT)	do
Tail Vehicle	15 cwt (MT repair)	do

Motor cycles (three) acted as route markers, marshallers and message carriers from me to the rest of the unit.

Notes * Out of gauge vehicles.
  ** Attached units' vehicles such as R/T point to point had their vehicles placed here.

Each vehicle had an RAF Type number and this is given where remembered.

APPENDIX 4

Itinerary

June 1944 to May 1945

11th June 1944	Land Normandy	'Love' Beach
12th June	Beaupigny	East of Bayeux
6th August	Foulanges	N of Caumont
17th August	La Villette	N of Condé sur Noire
24th August	Fontenai	15m S of Argentan
27th August	Grossoevres	Evreux
2nd September	La Vauroux	Beauvais
6th September	Melsbroek	Brussels
11th September	Velpen	Diest
21st September	Meeuwen	SW of Bree
26th September	Grave	Nr Nijmegen
8th October	Meeuwen	SW of Bree
11th March 1945	Bonninghardt	Opposite Wesel
13th April	Osnabruck	
16th April	Eschede	NE of Celle
19th April	Beedenbostel	NE of Celle
27th April	Horndorf	Lauenburg
6th May	Travemünde	NE of Lübeck

GLOSSARY

Call-sign	Each ground station and aircraft formation was allocated a call sign or name for identification purposes on the R/T
Clutter	Permanent radar responses from close ground or hills.
Compo Rations	The fourteen man one day pack of tinned rations. These came in eight varieties.
Echoes	Radar responses.
GCC	Group Control Centre responsible for the tasking and control of squadrons.
GCI	Ground Control Interception unit.
GSM	General Situation Map showing the air situation usually by means of plaques and arrows.
KENWAY	The call sign of the GCC, often used by aircrew to answer or as a reference to any ground control.
MEW	Mobile Early Warning. The initials MEW referred to the American radar site.
MT	Motor transport.
PPI	Plan Position Indicator. The console showing a map or plan position of a radar response.
RDF	Range and Direction Finding. Used as an early reference to what is now radar.
R/T	Radio Telephony.
Sector	The UK was divided into Groups for Air Defence. Each Group was divided into a number of areas called Sectors.
Trace	The line of light on the displays on which the aircraft responses appeared.
W/T	Wireless Telegraphy.